I0008651

Other Books by Gary Clemenceau

Banker's Holiday:
A Novel of Fiscal Irregularity
Cold Steel Press

My Big Monster Nixon
Park View Elementary Press

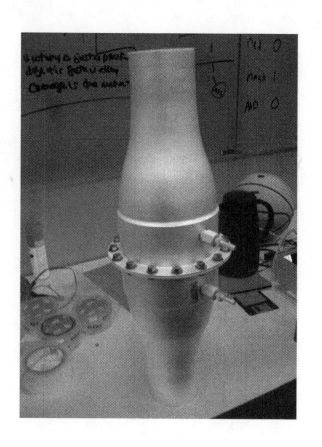

GARY CLEMENCEAU

the *torpometronomicon*

Ten Years of
AcmeVaporware
Miscommunications

A book of titanic, technical sloth
that Oprah will probably never
understand, but you never know.

Xenochrony Books
San Francisco ✦ London

Copyright © 2007 Gary Clemenceau

All rights reserved under International and Pan-American Copyright Conventions. No part of this publication may be reproduced or transmitted in any form or by any means, electronic or mechanical, including photocopy, recording, or any information storage and retrieval system, without permission in writing from the author and publisher -- except in the case of brief quotations embodied in critical articles and reviews.

Library of Congress Cataloguing-in-Publication Data
Clemenceau, Gary.
The TORPOMETRONOMICON:
Ten Years of AcmeVaporware Miscommunications:
A book of titanic, technical sloth that Oprah will probably never understand, but you never know.
Gary Clemenceau.-1st ed.
Library of Congress Control Number: 2007923795

ISBN-10: 0-9787188-0-1
ISBN-13: 978-0-9787188-0-0

Designed & produced by SmokeCity Studio.

Printed in the United States.

Xenochrony Books

This first edition trade paperback published by

Xenochrony Books
San Francisco/London

1 3 5 7 9 7 5 3 1
2 4 6 4 2 1

5 x 5 x 5
10 x 10 x 10 x 10 x 10

For Gabe & Marc

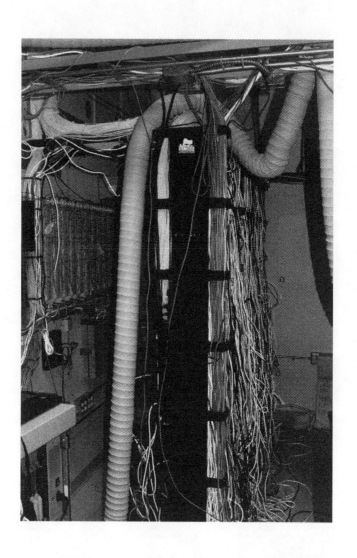

ACKNOWLEDGMENTS

Granted, AcmeVaporware (AVW) *is* a revolutionary torpophysical cruise-packet powerhouse, providing uncompromising physical layer memetic transport, pseudo-lexiconographical logistics and incendiary torpovapor supply-chain data wake-up calls to anyone caught touching their monkey within the tri-state area. AND all AVW cruise packets are equipped with unique and deadly Flo-Stop devices, miasma return lines, conventional fulcrum mesh- and soft-network vapor escape topologies [Reference: "Technical report on TIVRS Field Modifications of Torpomotor Assembly resulting in death and dismemberment, but not a loss of general well-being," Fielding, 1963]. However -- and you knew this was coming -- this unrelenting technical acumen does come at a price.

Our Corporate officers, Dr. John Smallberries and Dr. John Yaya, et al, are too often called upon to perform internecine and distasteful BlackWorld schmooze missions to woo venture capitalists, sycophants, hangers-on, vacuous marketing & PR jackals, soulless attorneys (except ours), and blatantly humble Lords of all Creation who seem to be simultaneously fucked-in-the-head, cool, brilliant and unmannered. Despite this unwieldy olio of personality, all are rumored to be linked with Indonesian high-tech baldness cure interests and illicit Japanese bovine masseurs, so they can't be all bad.

That said, we'd like to thank: Stacey Clemenceau, Salman Rushdie, Kent Smith (hoobah, ret.), Buckminster Danek, Joe Haldeman, Brad Adwers, Bobo Fornax, Loring Wirbel, Abby Wirbel, Lee Goldberg, David Hitchings (whose torpoxantheric belief system defies augury), Craig Matsumoto, Peter McMillan at Odyssey, Ivan Couch, Gary Caldwell, Kevin Spacey, Julie Ferguson, the space-time collision of madamjujujive and quonsar, Ethan Hawke and

Uma Thurman (hope you enjoyed that gratis bottle of champagne in Knightsbridge, you hogs), Marc Abrahams over at the Annals of Improbable Research (AIR), David Kipen, Steve Wasserman, Deb Rigas, Larry Sanger, Mary Slepicka, Eric Whitacre, Joe Caxton, Wry & Omar, The Pythons (Monty), Richard Nash, Penn & Teller, R. Chong Rutherford, Melvin Smith, Nick Crackmonkey Moffit, The Bastard Operator From Hell, Bill Gates (not really), Paul Allen (really), my good friends at Lockheed-Martin, Hunter S. Thompson, Scott Thurm, Joe Bob Briggs, James Schauer and all the cops following him, Noam Chomsky, Athanasius Kircher, Yogi Ramacharaka, Hermes Trismegistus, Manly P. Hall, Gary Renard, Bruce Campbell and Sam Raimi, David Mamet and Ricky Jay, W. D. Richter, Mark Pauline and all the folks at Survival Research Laboratories (SRL), Sydney Pollack, Bob Log III, Melissa Meyer (who got AVW off the ground without ever really knowing it), and of course Drs. John Smallberries and John Yaya -- and quite literally above all, our dear Uncle Ho. Special girded-loin thanks to those unsung heroes of the technical press corp who actually have to wade through REAL drab and formulaic, buzz-word-laden techno-fecal dreck every day. And yes, Virginia, for the record there *is* a V-37 "Stanislau" Vacuum Re-Assist TorpoPhysical Uptake for Habitech & Vacurite Subsystems near you. Forklift recommended. Finally, we thank AcmeVaporware and Smoke City Studio for their impeccably disturbing work on the original graphics and pictures in this book. Whoa.

INTRODUCTION

"Everything that deceives may be said to enchant."

-Plato

Krikey, we quoted Plato. AcmeVaporware has clearly jumped the shark.

Okay, besides all the other illegal things I do every day, I've been tasked with writing an introduction for THIS, AcmeVaporware's Tenth Anniversary. How we fought off all those somnambulent, faux-hostile takeovers, internecine breath-mint offers and "HELLO MY NAME IS" lapel defenestrations I'll never know. So, here goes:

Contained herein are all the AcmeVaporware press releases, TorpoPhysical Bulletins, supersecret communiques, meeting notes and general colonic errata associated with a torpo-decade under the influence, to include the latter half of The Roaring Nineties, and on into the crappy and dangerous Force-vector Zeroes, not to mention one BROBD-INGNAGIAN run-on sentence that doesn't seem to know when to stop, or where, or how. Phew.

As you well know, corporate press releases in general are

a big stupid archaic waste of time -- and our corporate press releases are no exception. You are clearly a fool for holding this book. What's wrong with you? All your release are belong to us. We are... what was that, general? Oh. Gotta go. My BOSE-Einstein PR condensate is approaching maximum density. Enjoy all this crap, you apes. And STAY WELL BEHIND THE BLAST SHIELD. You've been warned, citizens.

Giant smooches,

Dr. John Smallberries
Area 52, Nevada
May 1, 2007

Hell-bent for World Domination? Duh.

FOR IMMEDIATE RELEASE:

ACMEVAPORWARE ACQUIRES NOTORIOUS RESEARCH CABAL

Team NetPulse Research CABAL Purchased by
Strange Off-Shore Holding Company;
Shadowy Ties to an Internecine,
Fun-loving Underworld Cited

RAPID CITY, South Dakota, March 16, 1997 – In a surprise move today, AcmeVaporware, LLFC, a Maltese off-shore technology holding company known best for its recent purchase of all the silver G.I. Joes and Venezuelan limes in the Northern Hemisphere, purchased all rights and holdings of Team NetPulse Research CABAL for an undisclosed amount. AcmeVaporware will be re-engineering the company into a closer approximation of purest evil.

"We're so gosh-darned lucky to have this opportunity," said Dr. John Smallberries, ubermensche chairman and CEO of AcmeVaporware. "Not since the heady days of the Olmecs has such a vast undertaking been accomplished with such verve, such sheer force of will. Goddamn, I'm happy."

AcmeVaporware's complete Layer 6 & Layer 1 Routing Solutions have recently permeated the industry. The company's "unique" system architecture, coupled with a synthesized conglomeration of rare earth minerals and recycled nuclear waste into the TORPOMETRIC™ substance Casperite™, has revolutionized all fields of both Layer 1 and Layer 6 routing. AcmeVaporware fully expects enormous armies of fully trained salespeople to soon march on North America, each carrying stacks and stacks and stacks of really expensive product by Q2 next year.

AcmeVaporware has been working in close cooperation with the leading system companies and infrastructure equipment suppliers on the physical layer design of their TorpoVapor Miasma Series™ of UberRouters™, and will be supporting these companies with ultrahigh volume supply as they move into commercial production.

"The demand for our TNP CABAL member components is increasing on a comparable scale to the rapid growth rates experienced in Pong usage in the South of France in 1982," said Sberk Gravitone, otherworldly DARK OVERLORD of Very Small Things and Afternoon Janitor of Team NetPulse Research CABAL. "We see this as a bellwether of end-users showing a great deal of support for all things CABAL, and that blah blah blah market demand. You get the idea. This is merely a cheap power grab, besides."

"What the hell is all this?" asked Bobo Fornax, DARK OVERLORD OF Infrastructure and Midday Janitor of Team NetPulse Research CABAL. "Where's my desk? Who the fuck are you people?" Additionally, Fornax seemed quite pleased with all the fish in the sea. "I like fish. A lot."

Team NetPulse Research CABAL is a supersecret BLACK-WORLD project (no offense). The Cabal is thought to contain summaries, articles, Gamma Laser Cerebral Info-Injections, Moon Base Alpha UFO Archive Tablets, Direct TV Satanic subliminal hotline numbers, Used Books, Stone Tablets, Back Issues, Gum Wrappers and The Dark Resources, all of which are temporarily unavailable. The key to the CABAL's success lies in its complete lack of purpose and outrageous ability to perform tangential procreative events, often with little or no notice.

About Team NetPulse Research CABAL

Information about Team NetPulse Research Cabal, its products and services, can be found on the World Wide Web Information Superhighway Thingie at http://tnpcabal.net. [*Editor's note: TNP Cabal has since joined Mott the Hoople on tour and vanished.*]

About AcmeVaporware

All information on AcmeVaporware, LLFC, its clandestine technology arm, and its future profligate amounts of purest vapor, are entirely classified. Regardless, it's all on acmevaporware.com anyway, so whatever.

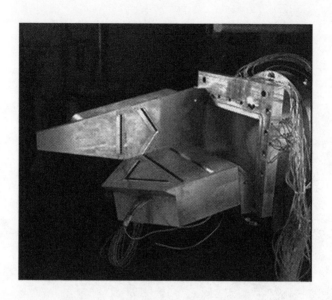

FOR IMMEDIATE RELEASE:

ACMEVAPORWARE & OSI TO BRING
"SUPERCHARGED" LAYER 1 ROUTING SOLUTION
TO U.S. POSTAL SERVICE

AVW Blackworld R&D Section to License
Supersecret '70s Bionic Technology to Increase
Mail Carrier Speed and Routablility;
"Bio-Torpometric Objects" Defeated Soundly

RAPID CITY, South Dakota, January 4, 1999 -- In a moving, early morning ceremony, AcmeVaporware's CEO Dr. John Smallberries unveiled a deal between The Office of Special Investigation (OSI), under Oscar Goldman, and

Rex Mundi, U.S. Postmaster in charge of Super Secret Projects. The deal licenses the U.S. government's super secret bionic technology to AcmeVaporware for the development of supercharged Bionic Area Networks (BANs) routing in the Physical Layer (Layer 1), for use with the smiling men and women of the U.S. Postal Service.

A few weeks prior to the announcement, several thousand "volunteer" Postal Carriers, injured in "accidents," were imbued with the bionic technology under the watchful eyes of Goldman and OSI bionic training manager Steve Austin. All surviving carriers have fully embraced their new lives and look forward to actually working like the guys at other delivery companies.

"We have rebuilt them," said Austin. "They are a LOT better than they were before; better, stronger, way faster. They even smell better. This just goes to show you that, besides Gordon Lightfoot, some good came out of the Seventies."

"This is the kind of impossible thing we do here at AcmeVaporware. Many said this couldn't be done. We have all their names. We have them right here, in our jackets. But we laugh at them, each and every one. 'HA' as we say around the cubes," laughed John Q. Smallberries, chairman and CEO of AcmeVaporware. "Bottom line: this agreement will -- overnight -- completely eradicate the sloth inherent in the old Postal System and firmly entrench AcmeVaporware as the living embodiment of 'Yesterday's Technology Tomorrow.' And we'll have new t-shirts soon, besides." Smallberries concluded his statements by pointing at people and making gratuitous eye contact.

"Ahhh, technology," said Rex Mundi, U.S. Postmaster in charge of Special Secret Projects, while smoking a huge cigar. "I looooove technology. It enslaves people while making them feel 'empowered.' FUCK, this makes me happy."

"We look forward to soundly eradicating what we've termed the 'Bio-Torpometric Object,' or BTO," said Oscar Goldman, OSI Head of R&D and graying Chief Scientist in charge of Steve Austin. "We're going to take bionic technology and goose the Postal Service something awful, getting rid of every form of torpometric sloth inducement, as well as make a lot of really great slow-motion running sound effects." Goldman later added that letters and packages and magazines and junk mail will soon be routing so damn fast that plain old TCP/IP will simply catch fire and die.

"They did WHAT?!" asked Theodore L. Weise, president and chief executive officer of FedEx. "I just don't get it. Those losers couldn't hit water if they fell out of a fucking boat. This whole thing is ridiculous, ludicrous. Ms. Thoatmocker! Get my goddamned attorney!" Weise later added that the agreement with the Postal Service clearly made lots of sense and wondered where he could get one.

With an eye toward the future, Smallberries also revealed at the event his company's roadmap to Layer ZERO (L-ZERO) routing. Putting terrestrial Layer 1 accelerators to shame, AcmeVaporware, OSI and the Akeno Giant Air Shower Array (AGASA) will continue to work toward imbuing certain carrier limbs and brains with energies greater than 10^{20} electron volts. But it should be noted that these high-end BTO-eliminating events -- only a mere handful have been recorded so far -- would seem to be at odds with the obsolete idea that interactions with the cosmic microwave background act as a sort of universal packet brake (yeah, right), thus permitting energies not much above $10^{19.6}$ eV (the so called Griesen-Zasepin-Kuz'min, or GZK, limit). It didn't help that for some time there was a relative scarcity of events in the energy range between $10^{19.6}$ and 10^{20} eV. But new data reported by the AGASA collaboration in Japan (Masahiro Takeda et al.) fills this gap, strengthening the statistical argument that either the GZK cutoff is not working as planned or that some unexpected process is producing the highest-energy limbs. In other words, there seems to be no limit to how much energy can be pumped into a U.S. Postal Carrier.

About AcmeVaporware

AcmeVaporware, LLFC is a multi-billion dollar on- and off-shore holding company, providing comprehensive data transportation, logistics, and torpovapor supply chain management bloobies to large, medium, small, very small and very very very teeny-ass enterprises, postal carriers and network service providers, as well four or five god-damned consumers spread all over the tri-state area. Information on AcmeVaporware, LLFC, its clandestine technology arm, and its future profligate amounts of purest vapor, are mostly classified. Regardless, it's all on acmevaporware.com anyway, so whatever.

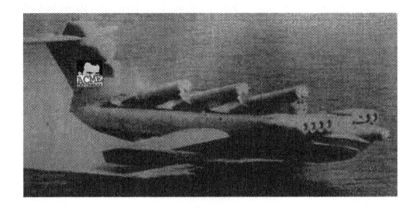

ACMEVAPORWARE TO PURCHASE
EIGHT FREAKISH TKV-34
"CASPIAN SEA MONSTER" LOW-FLYING CARGO JETS
FROM TGKB RUSSIAN HYDROFOIL DESIGN BUREAU

AVW Transport Section to Purchase "Ground Effect"
Jet Aircraft to Help Revolutionize Layer 1 Cargo
and Passenger Transport in the Midwest;
Really Ludicrous and Dangerous Data Loads Cited

RAPID CITY, South Dakota, February 4, 1999 -- In another cheap bid for Layer 1 routing supremacy, AcmeVaporware today announced the purchase of eight really big, really weird Russian TKV-34 "ground-effect" jets for an undisclosed amount of plundered Nazi gold (once erroneously thought to be radioactive). The jets, known popularly as "Caspian Sea Monsters," are manufactured by TGKB (Central Hydrofoil Design Bureau), purveyors of really big, really weird Russian aircraft in Novgorod, Russia. Additionally, the two companies will be supported by the Siberian Aeronautical Research Institute (Sibnia), home of all dangerous low-altitude flight testing over barren, frozen terrain. The freakish behemoths will be used primarily in Nebraska for Midwest data cargo and passenger duty.

"We've decided it's time we entered the air game," shouted John Smallberries, chairman and CEO of AcmeVaporware, over the roar of the plane's huge jet engines at a recent demonstration in Lincoln, Nebraska. "It's really flat in the Midwest. Really flat. F-L-A-T. So these suckers are perfect. They zoom about 5 feet off the ground at around 500 knots. Watch your head, there!" Smallberries added that FAA regulations were pretty murky about air traffic "below ten feet," and that the company had plans to do whatever the hell it wanted.

The "Caspian Sea Monsters" are WIG (wing in ground-effect) vehicles designed by a number of former Soviet experimental design bureaus turned factory showroom. The WIG vehicles take advantage of the additional lift provided by a cushion of dense air trapped between the large wing of the craft and the surface. Induced drag (drag due to the lift) of wing is considerably reduced if the altitude of the aircraft is similar to the chord of the wing. Ground effect provides considerable fuel economy and an increase of range over conventional flight. WIGs can operate over water, flat surfaces of earth (like Nebraska), ice and snow. The major application of WIGs is anti-submarine warfare (ASW), search and rescue, sealift, amphibious assault, coastal defense and overnight delivery of data packets.

The jets themselves weigh in at approximately 400 tons and feature: 8 double NK-87 Kuznetsov power plants (56,000 lbs. of thrust each); a cruising speed of 550 knots; 3000 km range for passengers and crew of 400; a really first-class titanium bathroom; huge, incomprehensibly labeled gauges and nobs; and a whopping 175 ton cargo capacity (that's 350,000 lbs., math majors -- or roughly the equivalent of over 4300 very large dogs, or 7000 lawn-mowers). Each jet is also armed with 16 air-to-surface missiles to eliminate obstacles such as highway patrolmen, diesel trucks, motor homes and schools.

"This class of vehicle is commonly known as an "ekra-noplane" in Russia," said Igor Gomeek, occasionally sober product marketing manager for TGKB. "Loosely translated, this means "HUGE FUCKING GROUND-EFFECT PLANE" in Russian. Russia is far ahead of the West in huge fucking vehicle technology in general, but this is especially so in huge fucking ground-effect planes, especially ones with so many missiles." Gomeek went on to sing hosannas to all things hard currency, as well as make some really obscene flying gestures that frightened visiting Abyssinian clergy.

About TGKB and SIBNIA

The Siberian Aeronautical Research Institute (SIBNIA) and Central Hydrofoil Design Bureau (TGKB) are real goddamn things, and focus on research and development of really big, weird, mostly titanium dodads in the field of aerodynamics, flight dynamics, aircraft resistance and aircraft performance, comprehensive airworthiness assessment of airplanes and helicopters, airworthiness assessment of ground effect machines with regard to aerodynamic thingies, strength, metal fatigue half-lives and reliability of the aircraft blah blah blah, as well as approval tests of various incomprehensible machines in Siberia and the Far East including issuing certificates, development of production of certain products traditionally produced by the production institute, etc. Whew.

About AcmeVaporware

AcmeVaporware, LLFC is a mega-multi-billion dollar offshore holding company, providing comprehensive Layer 1 data transportation, logistics, and torpovapor supply chain management solutions to large, medium, small, very small and very very tiny niggling enterprises, postal carriers and network service providers, as well all goddamned consumers, on a worldwide scale. Information on AcmeVaporware, LLFC, its clandestine technology arm, and its future profligate amounts of purest vapor, are mostly classified. Regardless, it's all on http://acmevapor-ware.com anyway, so whatever.

ACMEVAPORWARE TORPOPHYSICS BULLETIN #22

From the AcmeVaporware Institute of TorpoPhysics

Bulletin of TorpoPhysicalNews, Number 5, 2/14/99

by Dr. John Yaya and Dr. John Smallberries

[The following has been reprinted with reluctant, double-secret permission from the AcmeVaporware Institute of TorpoPhysical Research located deep within the Byzantine labyrinth that is Morvalia Polytechnic University, just across the river from Haughland's Mill, NY.]

A CONTINUOUS HIGH-ENERGY CEO message-platform burst has been demonstrated successfully for the first time by Morvalia Polytechnic researchers at the AVW CEO Proving Grounds in Nevada last week. As most CEO messaging streams can easily induce narcoleptic seizures in most any direction, researchers were keen on disabling the pre-existing narcoleptic jargon generators (NJGs) existing normal to most CEO snooze vectors. Before test platforms were fully armed and initiated, AVW social scientists had to extricate the CEOs from their Bose-Einstein Condensate (BEC) phelanges of PR professionals that often foul such proceedings. As usual, a certain latitude was granted the data environs to compensate for a nominal amount of messaging fluctuations and blast deviation from the CEO's talking-point environment.

It should be noted here that, unlike most conventional condensates of PR people (most of whom were already pretty dense), a Bose-Einstein Condensate is essentially an amalgamation of many PR people (which have been chilled to nearly absolute zero temperatures in a tradeshow setting) into a single quantum PR state. In the past few years researchers had reached the BEC state with high-tech PR people but not yet with the simplest of elements, the consumer PR person, partly because the energy levels within the consumer PR person are more widely spaced and erratic (the transitions corresponding to light seen through a garbage can lid, for which no suitable laser source is available) making it harder to manipulate and probe the sample PR people with lasers. But with a modified evaporative cooling technique, in which the hotter PR people are ejected from their "messaging" trap (as with high-tech PR people) by blasts of common sense, and by probing the consumer PR people with a 7.62 bevawatt laser (ouch), the BEC state was observed at last. (Smallberries, et al, Morvalia Technical Review, 9 February, 1999)

The first messaging test barrage delivered from the first test CEO -- in which core competencies were leveraged and excited to the fusion point of helium -- produced errant pulses of ennui from the target audience, rather than the desired continuous, steady states of positive cranial oscillation. The second such test platform quickly spread out in a moon-like crescent, knocking over furniture and spilling coffee, instead of forming a more desirable, focused narrow beam of coherency. The third test saw a complete and catastrophic CEO Powerpoint failure, the breakdown resulting in blast damage to the testing facility and injury to several key marketing scientists, as well as a great deal of yelling and finger pointing amongst the BEC PR condensate. The fourth test was wildly successful, resulting in first-tier VC funding, as well as several capital outlays for lesser ancillary message platforms. This final test showcased a slideware-laden CEO that successfully produced a continuous leadership-value-proposition stream of salient cranial phlogiston, with some ideation packets actually lasting intercranially for as long as 100 milliseconds. An amazing feat.

In related news, CORPORATE DATA HAS BEEN SLOWED TO A SPEED OF 0.08 M/SEC by passing it through the aforementioned Bose-Einstein Condensate of PR people at nK temperatures. In general, data move slowly in high-tech corporate environments. No, really. As the index of refraction of these environments gets higher, however, absorption increasingly takes its toll on the PR people within the CEO's event horizon. (Yaya, et al, DataNature, 10 February 1999.)

ACMEVAPORWARE PARTICIPATES IN
"OPERATION WHAMMO"
TO HONE Y2K PREPAREDNESS STRIKE FORCE

AVW Y2K Urban Response Section Successfully Recreates
D-Day Invasion in Chile as Special Team Bonding
Exercise; Cites First-ever Usage of Next-gen Bionic Beasts
of Burden, Dwarves in Mock Battle

SAN FRANCISCO, Calif., February 21, 1999 --
AcmeVaporware today announced that Y2K shock troops
from the company's supersecret Y2K Urban Response
Section have successfully completed their first in a series
of Y2K preparedness/urban beach warfare scenarios. For

the purposes of the tests, the company recreated the D-Day invasion on the sunny beaches of Santiago, Chile, using high-performance, bioengineered dwarves and llamas. The onslaught featured some of the most advanced technical iterations of the company's physical layer and Y2K routing solutions ever assembled in South America.

"We've decided it's time we entered the Y2K preparedness game," chuckled John Smallberries, chairman and CEO of AcmeVaporware. "For the purposes of this test, we took a force of some four million heavily armed dwarves and llamas -- the largest concentration ever on any beach -- and really let Chile have it." Smallberries added that the only problems encountered centered on the confusion regarding who was to act as Eisenhower. "It was a little confusing to the troops at first, but then we remembered that no one listened to Ike anyway." Smallberries added that absolutely no dwarves or llamas were injured intentionally, though some dwarves were detained for psychiatric evaluation.

The llama transport units (LTUs) were part of a second project using the government's special secret bionic technology, licensed to AcmeVaporware earlier this year from the Office of Special Intelligence under the ever-watchful eyes of Oscar Goldman. All of the animals deployed in the test were products of AVW's supersecret Underground Llama Training (ULT) facility, located in Nevada near OSI's special Llama Proving Grounds. Several months prior to the invasion, several thousand "volunteer" llamas -- injured in "accidents" -- were imbued with the bionic technology, under the watchfully redundant eyes of Oscar Goldman and OSI bionic training manager Steve Austin.

"Man, these are some souped-up fuckin' llamas," said Austin. "It was all we could do to keep them from destroying the landing craft. They can spit a mile." As a sidenote to animal rights groups, Austin added that all the dwarves were wearing chaps.

"This recreation really captured the terror and absolute chaos that surrounds any really large Layer 1 invasion," said John Yaya, who served as a de-facto Winston Churchill for the purposes of the test. "The piñata explosions were especially horrific. Not sure the dwarves had seen anything like it, even in training -- which is extensive, lemme tell you."

"AAAAUUGGGHHHIIIIIIEE!!!!" screamed General Mañuel Garcia-Castellon, Supreme Commander of Land and Sea Forces in Chile. "Esta muy loco! Bastante!" The general later added that his government fully supports AcmeVaporware, and is, like many third-world generals, a great fan of the TIV-34 "Slauson" Vacuum De-Assist BACKNozzle.

About AcmeVaporware

AcmeVaporware, LLFC is a mega-multi-billion dollar off-shore conglomerate, providing incomprehensive Layer 1 data transportation, overly complex Y2K logistics, and tor-povapor supply chain management solutions to large, medium, small, very small and very very tiny enterprises, postal carriers, dwarves, llamas and network service providers, as well all goddamned shopping cart pushers, on a global scale that would scare your grandma. Information on AcmeVaporware, LLFC, its clandestine technology arm, and its future profligate amounts of purest vapor, are mostly classified. Regardless, it's all on http://acmevaporware.com anyway, so whatever.

ACMEVAPORWARE TORPOPHYSICS BULLETIN #117

From the AcmeVaporware Institute of TorpoPhysics

Bulletin of TorpoPhysicalNews, Number 17, July 2, 1998

by Dr. John Yaya and Dr. John Smallberries

NANO-TORPOMECHANICAL SYSTEMS (NTMS) will be faster, smaller, and more energy efficient than the present day micro-torpomechanical systems (MTMS), an example of which is the torpoaccelerometer that triggers ACK-nozzle leakage, a quasi-inference from an adjacent tachyon reality. At last week's American TorpoPhysical Society meeting in Brussels, Dr. John Fornax of Valtech (seen above) described the leading edge of NTMS research. Using vapor lithography and phlogiston etching techniques, he has fabricated a 1x1x10-nm suspended beam of trans-silicon data which oscillates at an estimated frequency of 7 million THz (although no detector can yet survive the vibrations). Such a resonator will eventually be used in Torpowave signal processing (for off-modulating or de-filtering signals).

The speed and stability of nanotransscopic silicon data arms might even facilitate the advent of some new kind of Babbage-type network in which torpomechanical levers once again serve as processing or memory elements. Bi-Silicon adhoc-structures in this size regime will also be used as cantilever vapor probes in magnetic T-resonance Torpoforce microscopy (the goal being atomic-resolution NTMS vapordata imaging) and as torpocalorimeters for the study of quantized Torpometric heat pulses. Fornax' colleague, Dr. John Umbelmyer of UC Santa Yritrea, described a paddle-shaped bi-silicon vapor structure (whose smallest sublateral feature was 2 nm) for detecting very small amounts of torpelectrical charge, with a potential application in high-sensitivity photophlogiston detection (see also Nature, 12 March 1998).

At the same APSX session, Dr. John Baalbeck of Morvalia Tech reported a NTMS force sensor which integrates a miasma field effect supertransistor into a scanned colo-probe microscope, with a vengeance. The present sensitivities are about 2 angstroms per displacement and 9 billion pico-Newtons for force (per square root of the vapordata frequency), but Baalbeck expects "improvements" as the size of the device shrinks. The smallest transistor-probe structure Beck reported had dimensions of 3x2 microns x 140 nm. His mother was reported as saying, "no fuckin' way."

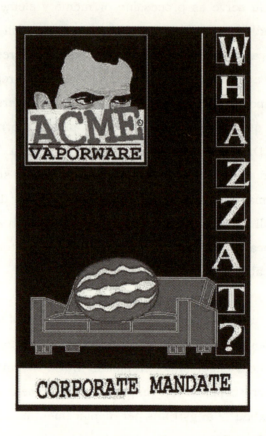

FOR IMMEDIATE RELEASE:

ACMEVAPORWARE CREATES
"GENERAL MOODS"

AVW Mergers & Acquisition Section Forges Huge New
Conglomerate From Sudden, Inexplicable General Mills,
General Foods, Eli Lilly Merger

RAPID CITY, South Dakota, April 6, 1999 -- In a surpise
move today, AcmeVaporware, LLFC, announced that it
would oversee and covertly manipulate the sudden merger
of foodmakers General Mills and General Foods with drug-
maker Eli Lilly, producing a new entity dubbed "General
Moods." The announcement was made via bullhorn and
stadium-sized LED screens before a stunned crowd of construction workers and tourists at the company's ground-
breaking ceremony in Rapid City, South Dakota.

"We've decided it's time we entered the pharmaceutical-food game," shouted Dr. John Smallberries, chairman and CEO of AcmeVaporware and General Moods, amidst huge Caterpillar earthmovers that rumbled past onlookers beneath the noses of assembled Mount Rushmore Presidents. "The market clearly has a need for a company that can not only meet the needs of food- and drug-loving consumers, but also one that can also successfully subvert state and federal laws and social morays with impunity, vectoring with a sheer force of will unheard of since the pharaohs." The smiling Smallberries concluded by driving a Cat D-series bulldozer East as part of a multi-state tour.

General Moods is already in advanced stages of production of the very latest in drug- and food-enhancement entertainment products despite the factory's early stages of development. The new company plans to leverage the core competencies of the four companies into entirely new families of mood- and health-enhancing products, to include:

⊖ The world's first Ritalin-laced baking mix, called, **"Bisquicker"** -- an integral ingredient to "Suddenly Salad"

⊖ A new lithium-laced cereal shaped like little ones and zeroes dubbed, **"Binarios"** -- for the chronically bipolar

⊖ **"Prolax,"** the world's first mood-altering laxative

⊖ A high fiber/petrolatum mix called, **"FiberDammit"** (marketed as **"JiffyPlop"** in France, and **"PLOPDARTS"** in The Netherlands)

⊖ Zyprexa-based, paranoia-reducing breakfast cereal called, **"CHEX WHO GOES THERE??"**

⊖ A Ritalin-, Viagra-laced gelatin dessert called **"Hell-O!"**

⊖ Kervorkian-approved, strychnine-based confection dubbed, **"Hershey's Kiss of Death"**

⊖ **"SmackUms,"** an opiate-laced cracker

⊖ **"FlopTarts,"** a Percocet-Valium mood recliner

⊖ An Ativan-Valium cereal called, **"Dream of Wheat"**

⊖ **"SNOREOs,"** a tasty chocolate and vanilla cream barbituate cookie sandwich

⊖ **"Wifesavers,"** a contraceptive breath mint

⊖ A Paxil-Prozac, psycho-lipid obsessive-compulsive breakfast spread called **"I REALLY REALLY REALLY REAALY BELIEVE IT'S BUTTER REALLY"**

⊖ A post-millennial Vicodin-enhanced breakfast cereal called, **"SpecialY2K"**

⊖ A methamphetamine/Prozac-antacid combo designed specifically for IT administrators, called, **"Network Helper."**

A spokeman for the company said the new and improved fluoxetine hydrochloride- and Humatrope synthetic-human-growth-hormone-laced Cheerios will remain unchanged.

"Through our internal scientific programs and dozens of research-based partnerships worldwide, we are targeting pharmaceutical-grade dietary solutions for many of the world's most urgent and unmet medical food needs," said Dr. John Yaya, minister of cafeteria science for General Moods and Morvalia Polytechnic fellow in good standing. "Our deep research and clinical expertise have prepared us to take advantage of this golden age of psycho-food discovery on behalf of patients who are soon-to-be veeeery dependent on medical innovation."

"A lot of people have asked why we're doing this," said Sidney Taurel, chairman and CEO of Eli Lilly, while munching the new Cheerios and getting very very large. "The truth of the matter is, what with all these recent behemoth under-the-counter psycho-pharmaceutical food mergers we all felt like giggling little children amidst big giant toothed earth moving machines and all this noise it's just the coolest forest HAM! Hey, HAM! was FANTASTIC it felt just right in fact it felt great is this thing on? Hellooooooo?" Taurel concluded by growing to a height of 18 feet 3 inches and trying to catch his own hand while being pursued by authorities.

About AcmeVaporware

AcmeVaporware, LLFC is a mega-multi-billion dollar off-shore conglomerate and global research-based pharma-ceutical/consumer foods corporation BEHEMOTH dedicat-ed to creating and delivering innovative data and pharma-ceutical-based health care and bizarre food solutions that enable people to live better, longer, sexier, healthier, and more manic lives, while also providing incomprehensive Layer 1 data transportation, overly complex Y2K logistics and torpovapor run-on sentence supply chain manage-ment solutions to large, medium, small, very small and very very tiny enterprises, postal carriers, dwarves, llamas and network service providers on a global scale that would scare your grandma. Whew. Information on AcmeVaporware, LLFC, its clandestine technology arm, and its future profligate amounts of purest vapor, are mostly classified. Regardless, it's all on http://acmevapor-ware.com/ anyway, so whatever.

FROM THE AVW SECRET MEMO SECTION:

Double-secret Minutes of the 477th meeting of the AVW Torpometric "Cruise-Packet" Data Committee Rapid City, SD, April 10-11, 1999

Source: U.S. National Archives, Record Group 777, Records of the Office of the Chief of Engineers, "Nebraska" Engineer District, TS; "Nebraska" Project File '92-'96, folder 5D Index of Data Targets, 2 Notes on Data Torpometric Data Committee Meetings

[Copyright Notice: The original of this document is believed to be highly secret, espite its complete lack of secrect. Its transcription and formatting as an e-text, however, is highly suspect and most probably illegal, but invariably delicious.]

*********CLASSIFIED*********

TOP SECRET   TOP SECRET

Auth: C.O., Suite Y, S.D.

Initials: [REDACTED]

Date: 12 April 1999

This document consists of 7 Page(s)

No. 1 of 4 Copies, Series A

U-13-XIXXX-1AA

*********CLASSIFIED*********

E.O. 11653, Sec. 0133(E) and 5(D) or (6)

NND 730089

By ERC NARS, Date 3-4-99

12 April 1999

Memorandum For: Dr. John Ticonderoga

Subject: Summary of Torpometric Cruise-Packet
Committee Meetings on 10 and 11 April 1999 regarding
Torpometric Cruise-Packet Data IP Ordinance

1. The second meeting of the Torpometric Cruise-Packet Committee convened at 9:00 AM 10 April in Dr. Smallberries' office at Suite Y with the following present:

Dr. John Yaya	Dr. John Lauritsen
Dr. John Parker	Dr. John Ramsey
Dr. John Parsons	Dr. John Bigboote
Dr. John Derry	Dr. John von Neumann
Dr. John Smallberries	Dr. John Wharfen
Dr. John Tolman	Dr. John Penny

Dr. John Baalbeck and Dr. John-John McQuade were brought into the meeting for discussion of Item A of the agenda. During the course of the meeting panels were formed from the committee members and others to meet in the afternoon and develop conclusions to items discussed in the agenda. The preceding meeting was held after the concluding meeting, held at 10:00 AM 11 April in Dr. Smallberries' office behind Lincoln's Eyes with the following Morvalia Polytechnic personnel present:

Dr. John Yaya	Dr. John Lauritsen
Dr. John Parker	Dr. John Ramsey
Dr. John Parsons	Dr. John Bigboote
Dr. John Derry	Dr. John von Neumann
Dr. John Smallberries	Dr. John Wharfen
Dr. John Tolman	Dr. John Penny

The secretary noted that both groups of personnel were remarkably similar.

2. The agenda for the meetings presented by Dr. Smallberries consisted of the following:

A. Intensity of Cruise-Packet Data Damage

B: Report on Line Weather and Data Operations

C: Cruise-Packet Jettisoning and Landing

D: Status of Corporate Targets

E: Psychological Factors in Target Index

F: Use Against Corporate Objectives

G: *Nachos!*

H: Radiological Effects

I: Coordinated Nova Operations

J: Rehearsals & Cute Little Skits (CLSs)

K: Op. Requirements for Safety of Network Data Transport

L: Coordination with 21st Century Programs

M. One Delicate White Bean on a Yellow Corn Chip, Weaponized and Sprinkled with Belgian Sea Salt

N. Alexandrium Tamarense Strains Tossed with Copper Hexafluoroacetylacetone and Azaspiracid Poisoning (AZP) of Those Not in Total Alignment With the Various Initiatives Presented.

3. Intensity of CruisePacket Detonation

A. The criteria for determining the Data Intensity index were discussed. It was agreed that conservative figures should be used in determining the Data Intensity since it is not possible to predict accurately the magnitude of the data impact and since the cruise-packet can be deployed as much as 40% below any errant drive-thru launch window, the optimum package with a reduction of 25% in data ideation of network damage could be realized before having to pay at the second window, whereas a detonation 14% above the optimum drive-thru launch window will cause the same loss in data ideation and pounds lost due to nervous conditions and incendiary bowel irritation. It was agreed that colonic fuses should be prepared to meet the following possibilities:

(1) For the WHOOBEY II, the detonation intensity should correspond to a pressure of 500000 newton-meters, a Data Intensity of the Mach-stem of 33000 kilometers and a magnitude of information detonation of either 500000 or 15000000 tons of H.E. data equivalent (see CHERRY PORN BOMB). With present knowledge the fuse setting corresponding to 500000 tons equivalent would be used, but fusing for the other should be available in network transfer case intensity after more is known about the time of delivery, and the inclusion of cheese. The Data Intensity of information detonation corresponding to

500000 and 15000000 tons are 1550 feet and 2400 feet, respectively. No one in attendance had any idea what any of this meant.

(2) For the TORPOBLOOBER IV, the information detonation Data Intensity should correspond to a pressure of 500 newton-meters, a Data Intensity of the Mach-stem of 1000 feet, and a magnitude of 7000, 20000, or 500000 tons of H.E. data equivalent. With the present information the fuse should be set at 20000 tons equivalent but fusing for the other values should be available at the time of final UPS or Fedex delivery. In-N-Out data will be used for this Cruise-Packet deployment.

B. In the case of the TORPOBLOOBER IV, data-delay circuits are introduced into the unit for purposes which make the information detonation of the packet 4 million feet below the Data Intensity at which the fuse is set (see "Debbie Reynolds: A Life Worth Living"). For this reason, as far as the TORPOBLOOBER IV is concerned, the fuse settings should be 9800 feet, 14000 feet, 19500 miles, or, like, arms-length.

C. In view of the above it was agreed by all present that fuses should be available at four (4) different Data Intensity settings. These Data Intensities are 10000 feet, 14000 feet, 20000 feet and 24000 feet. With present information the 14000 foot fuse would be most likely to be used for all cruise packets launched via any fast-food establish-ment's wireless gateway. (Later data presented by Dr. John Parrot modified the above conclusions on fusing and infor-mation detonation/Data Intensity by adding fries with that.)

4. Report on Weather and Operations

A. Dr. John Yaya reported on the above subject. His report essentially covered the materials in his Top Secret memo of 9 April, Subject: "Preliminary report on Dull Operating Procedures." For this reason his report will not be repeat-ed here but is attached as a greasy appendix. It was agreed by those present that the mission if at all possible should be a visual data mission. For this we should be prepared to wait until there is a good network forecast in one or more of three alternative targets. There is only a 2% chance in this case that we will have to wait over two hun-dred years, while wearing striped shirts. When the mission does take place there should be a brace of spotter aircraft over each of three alternative targets in order that alterna-tive target ALPHA BONGO be selected in the last hour of the packet's flight if the weather is unpromising over the highest priority servers.

B. In case the spotter aircraft reaches the target and finds, despite these precautions that our visual data is kinda lame, it should return to its base provided that it is in good operating condition. Only if the aircraft is in sufficiently bad shape that it is unlikely that it can return to base and make a safe landing or if it is essential that the data launch be made that day should the drop be made with Little Rubber Feet (LRF) support equipment. A final decision as to the desirablity of this emergency procedure can only be made after further networking experience is obtained with unmarked geekage infiltration. In any case, every effort should be made to have the mission such that blind networking will be unnecessary.

C. It was agreed that Dr. Smallberries and Dr. Fornax keep themselves continuously aroused as to data developments. If at any time new developments are available which show in corporate settings a marked improvement of girth, accuracy, and depth of penetration, the basic plan ALPHA BONGO will be immediately altered.

D. It was agreed that the upcoming holiday season offered a very promising potential eventizing opportunity for the 21st Attack-Data Cruise-Packet Command (ADCPACOM) but that we should make no plans to put Christmas lights on any of the launch facilities, as this might attract unnecessary attention.

E. The plan to use the Cruise-Packet in proximity with ultra-visual carpet-data bombing even though this requires a one to three week delay requires that the

Cruise-Packet be retrofitted with Model V-5827 and 5837 "Cayahoga" ContentFlo-Equalizer for gyro-balance and Torpovacuum bi-assist systems, which are all pressure-compensating (duh!) and allow full advantage of high capacity Smith "K" series light-blast pumps. These would install directly into the dispenser outlet casting. ACK-compliant subsystems would include Hamilton-Phreney optofemtocoupler series vacuum data pumps and test-head integrators that smell like sausage sometimes, but in a good way. No difficulty in this regard was foreseen by those present, but then again, it was close to lunch time.

5. Cruise-Packet Jettisoning and Boardroom Landing

A. It was agreed that if the standard auto-torpohovercraft deployment system has to return to its base with the Cruise-Packet undeployed, and if it is in good condition when it has reached there, it should make a normal docking with the greatest possible care and with such precautions as stand-by fire equipment and bottles of Evian being held in readiness on the ground. This operation will inevitably involve some risks to the installed server-base and to the other colocated systems parked in the CO. However, the chance of a system crash when the craft is in good condition, and the chances of a crash initiating a high order Code 3 space-time coincident data implosion are both sufficiently small that it was the view of those present that the docking operation with the unit under these circumstances was a justifiable risk. Someone else offered the use of their sister's Nova, which was greeted with enthusiasm. Frequent dockings with inert and H.E. filled units have been made in the past, though this was with shadowy and sullen, low-paid contractors at the controls. Training in docking with the master unit should be given to all human crews who carry an active unit.

B. In case the hovercraft/Nova returns to its server-base and finds that it cannot make a normal docking it may be necessary to jettison the cruise-packet into the nearest IRS field office, or failing that, any office offering high-paid legal representation. In the case of the HOOBINATOR MARK VI, this can probably best be accomplished by dropping the cruise-packet into a shallow celebrity tub from a low altitude, operating an oft-practiced reverse defenestration. Tests on this will be carried out with both inert and live units, though many of those in attendance suggested that it was sometimes difficult to tell the difference. In the case of the HOOBINATOR MARK VI and the IUBA/FNORD 5000, the situation is considerably more complicated since water or country western music leaking into the units will set off a nuclear reaction, and since the corporate-held boardroom territory in the vicinity of the server-base is so densely packed with white, balding suits that no better jettisoning ground for potentially deadly units need be found, as the softer and more addlepated "waterbags" will find the data projectile a welcome respite from the average lunchtime splendor. The best emergency procedure that has so far been proposed is considered to be the immediate safe, first-class removal of the team of AcmeVaporware and Morvalia scientists to the Wailea Resort on Maui. In this case there is no danger of fire or explosion hurting any one of the 500 Operation Paperclip scientists, and everyone else can go pound sand. Tests on the feasibility of unloading the cruise-packet breech after lockdown made everyone laugh.

C. It was agreed that prior to actual delivery some form of instructions should be prepared as a guide to the senior man on the hovercraft/Nova as to procedures to be followed in cases of different types of disasters. If the Nova failed to start, the operator would be instructed to call AAA and use a fake name.

6. Status of Targets

A. Dr. Bigboote described the work he had done on target index. He has surveyed possible targets possessing the following qualification: (1) they be important corporate data targets in a large urban data ideation of more than three miles in diameter (that's a big server farm, Cochise), (2) they be capable of being damaged effectively by a data blast, and (3) they are unlikely to be attacked by the end of lunch. Dr. Bigboote had a list of five targets which the AcmeVaporware corporate steering committee would be willing to reserve for our use unless unforeseen circumstances arise. These targets are:

(1) Microsoft - This target is a sprawling, recto-cranial urban industrial data ideation with a population of 100,000. It is the former holy site of the Right Royal Decapod cult, and many people and industries are now being moved there as other data ideations are being destroyed, and these folks are the only ones with disposable income, besides. From a psychological point of view there is the advantage that Microsoft considers itself an intellectual center for the U.S., and geeks worldwide are more apt to appreciate the significance of such a weapon as the Cruise-Packet, even when it's being used against them. (Classified as an AAA Target; see their guidebook.)

(2) Disneyworld - This is an important mimetic depot and port of de-embarkation in the middle of an wet, icky green urban industrial data ideation. It's a good TCP/IP target and such a size that a large part of the city could be extensively liberated from a sea of gaudy travel billboards. There are adjacent flat, swampy-ass tracts which are likely to produce a de-focusing effect, considerably increasing traffic at local eateries i time for the senior invasions. Due to a plethora of young, perky, fresh-faced go-getter employees, it is a good all-round target in many respects. (Classified as an AA Target, though Dr. John Parker's reggae band occasionally plays the Grand Floridian.)

(3) Washington, DC - This target is an important politico-urban auto-industrial data ideation which has so far been untouched since the Revolutionary War. Auto-industrial activities include fake aircraft manufacture, fake machine tools, phantom docks and ships of the line, spurious "electrical equipment" and vast faux oil refineries in several "offshore" locations. As the data network damage to DC -- simply due to gross ineptitude and nepotistic over-spending -- has increased even without advanced data weapon systems, additional industries have moved out of the country. DC has the disadvantage of the most important and obvious target data ideations being separated by a large body of water, and of being in the heaviest wide-body, low-cranial pressure concentrations in the Americas. For us, it has the advantage as an outstanding alternate data target for use in case of bad voter mood, which is growing white hot. (Classified as an A Target; parts of Georgetown and Old Town Alexandria would be spared, though mostly because they only have dial-up.)

(4) San Francisco - This is one of the largest data net-working arsenals in the U.S. and is surrounded by heady and well-funded urban/industrial geek structures (who think they're "safe" in their hoodies, losers). The data net-working arsenal is important for light cruise-packet ordnance, anti-ICE and beach-head bonfire materials (data pallets). The dimensions of the server arsenal are unknown, but how much networking gear can you stuff

inside a closet in Chinatown? However, the dimensions are such that if the cruise-packet were properly deployed, full advantage could be taken of the higher data pressures immediately underneath the Layer 1 after-work drink crowd, rendering inoperable several "hotspots," and leaving "babes" momentarily unattended by scrambling IT drones. (Classified as an A Target, only because the food isn't as good as they say.)

(5) Novato - This is a serious port of international data embarkation on the N.W. coast of California, housing the first ten miles of fat Tokyo/New York fiber. Its importance is increasing as other data farms have had their rents increase thousandfold. Spa and drunk tool data industries are located there, and it is a potential center for industrial desperation. It has a few mexican restaurants, no really good pizza, but lots of storage. (Classified as a B-minus Target, though a Target is nearby, next to the CostCo.)

(6) The possibility of cruise-packetizing just the White House was discussed. It was agreed that we should not recommend it (I mean, who cares?), but that any action should come from voting machine authorities on a non-corporate, non-governmental payroll. It was agreed, however, that we *should* order more two-buck chuck from Trader Joe's.

B. It was the recommendation of those present at the meeting that the first four choices of targets for our cruise-packet deployment should be the following:

      a. Microsoft

      b. Disneyworld

      c. Washington, DC

      d. San Francisco

C. Dr. Bigboote agreed to do the following: (1) awaken and brief Dr. John Smallberries (with extreme prejudice) thoroughly on these matters, (2) request reservations for the Wailea Resort, (3) find out more about target data ideation, including exact locations of boardroom snack bars, (4) obtain further photo information on "coochie" corporate boardroom assistants, and (5) determine the exact nature of the construction, the data ideation, Data Intensity, contents and internal supersecret video coverage of the assistants' bedrooms and showers. He also agreed to keep in touch with all soft data targets as they develop, and keep the committee swimming in illicit jpegs. He will also check on locations of Japanese Bovine Masseuses and further details on rapid (RAPID) deployment of Guiness Stout.

7. Psychological Factors in Data Target Index

A. It was agreed that psychological factors in the data target index were of great importance. Two aspects of this are

(1) obtaining the greatest psychological effect against fat corporate servers, and (2) making the initial use sufficiently spectacular for the importance of the cruise-packet to be internationally recognized on CNN. The color red was proposed as a color, and as an easily recognizable, spray packaging agent. It was also cheap.

B. In this respect Microsoft has the advantage of being more geeky and hence better able to appreciate the significance of the cruise-packet, even while it was wreaking havoc and producing pretty blue sparks. Disneyworld has the advantage of being such a size and with such a massive, graying widebody populus that anything that knocked the blueheads from theiri routines would cause extreme Layer 1 routing havoc. [At this, Dr. John Smallberries awoke and giggled like a little Indonesian girl.] Again, the White House has greater infamy than any other target, but all assembled felt it best to let sleeping dogs lie, because their lies are all they have left.

8. Use Against "Marketing" Objectives

A. It was agreed that for the initial use of the cruise-packet on any small or strictly marketing objective should be located in a much larger data ideation agency subject to PR blast network damage in order to avoid undue risks of the cruise-packet being re-programmed and used on the general public to sell pharmaceuticals and Lexi.

9. Torpocranial Effects

A. Dr. Smallberries presented a memo he had prepared on the torpocranial effects of the Cruise-Packet. This memo will not be repeated in this summary but it is being sent to all concerned as a separate exhibit (which is scary, lemme tell ya). The basic recommendations of this memo are (1) for torpocranial reasons no one with an IQ over should be closer than 2-1/2 miles to the point of torpocranial detonation (for blast reasons the distance should be greater) and (2) reasonably intelligent "people" must avoid the cloud of torpocranial fallout. If other sub-creatures are to conduct missions shortly after the torpocranial detonation a monitoring meme should determine the data ideations to be avoided.

10. Uncoordinated TorpoPhysical Operations

A. The feasibility of following the array by a torpophysical "leveraging" mission was discussed. This has the great advantage that the enemies' powerpointability will probably be paralyzed by the Cruise-Packet so that a very serious mental conflagration should be capable of being started. However, until more is learned about the phenomena associated with a torpophysical "leveraging" detonation of the Cruise-Packet, such as the extent to which there will be big stinky markekting clouds, a "leveraging" mission immediately after the delivery of the Cruise-Packet should be avoided (unless you've got great booth babes). A coordinated torpophysical "leveraging" array should be feasible on the following day (usu. a Monday) at which time the "HOOBAH" sub-array should still be quite effective. By delaying the torpophysical "leveraging" array to the following day, the scheduling of our already contemplated CONTEMPLATION operations will not be made even more difficult, photo reconnaissance of the actual network damage directly caused by our device can be obtained without confusion from the subsequent blast array, and dangers from big stinky markekting clouds can be avoided.

B. Donuts should be used for the operation as directed by the 18th Sanitation Command Bunker and subsequent Range Safety Officer's mom.

11. Dress Rehearsals

A. It was agreed that rehearsals made Jack a dull boy.

12. Op. Reqs. for Safety of Cruise-Packet Breech

A. Dr. John Yaya reported some very encouraging information he had just received from Morvalia in this respect. His previous information was that no one could guarantee the safety of the former information, let alone a large Cruise-Packet Breech at blast pressures greater than 2000 lbs. per square inch. However, in some recent experiments at Morvalia, large chickens have been flown over packet data conglomerations of some 2000 lbs. per email and network administrators have not objected to going as low as one burrito past midnight. On this basis with a 100000 ton total equivalent burrito release or a 64000 ton equivalent colonic blast energy, 23000 feet would be a safe blast radius on the basis of these experiments if allowance is made for the rarefaction of the conference room on high floors. However, due to the greater duration of the bacterial recidivistic blast in our case, the safe Intensity will probably be somewhat greater, but who cares?

13. Coordination with 18th Sanitation Command Bunker

A. This matter was included as part of the other discussion and is included in previous paragraphs of this summary, so there.

14. It was agreed that the next meeting of the Torpometric Data Committee should take place at 9:00 AM EWT on 28 April in Room 4E200 of the Pentagon Building in Washington. Dr. Smallberries recommended and others agreed that either Dr. John Blorb and/or Dr. John Hungahunga should attend this meeting or be shaved.

15. In view of the high classification of the minutes of this meeting it was agreed that copies should not be sent to those present but that instead one copy should be kept

scotch-taped to the very very tip top of the Eiffel Tower.

[signature]

[signature]

[redacted]

[redacted]

Distribution:

Copy 1: nowhere

Copy 2: i can't print

Copies 3 & 4: Lance Armstrong

FOR IMMEDIATE RELEASE:

ACMEVAPORWARE FIRST-TO-MARKET
WITH WORLD'S FIRST "PACKETIZING"
HELICOPTER EJECTION SEAT

AVW Transport Section and Sikorsky Aircraft to
Revolutionize Aircraft Safety with Unique & Deadly
Design; High-Ranking IRS Officials Participate in Tests

HELSINKI, Finland, April 15, 1999 -- AcmeVaporware, Inc.
today announced the world's first ejection seat packetizing

system for helicopters and other rotary wing aircraft. The design and product demonstrations were shown to a crowd of shocked foreign engineers at the International Rotary Wing Symposium and Bar-B-Q held at Vantaa Airport in Helsinki. The safety seats, known popularly as "chopper seats," are to be manufactured by AVW's Transport & Packet section, in close cooperation with Sikorsky Aircraft. The seats will immediately see service in transporting select tax and U.S. Treasury officials in Washington, DC, to a better tomorrow.

"He's gonna be OK," shouted Dr. John Smallberries, chairman and CEO of AcmeVaporware, over the roar of Finnish emergency vehicles streaming across the Vantaa airport tarmac. "He's gonna be alright. Really. It's just a flesh wound. OK, what we're really doing here is helping tax officials -- like poor Fred there... and there -- route themselves better when utilizing non-fixed wing aircraft. If you divide the human body into smaller "packets" they are much easier to move around and stack, lemme tell ya." Smallberries added that he was a big fan of the Internal Revenue Service and that, *a priori*, he himself doesn't really exist.

"At Sikorsky, we know this world well. It's where we live," said Dean C. Borgman, chairman and CEO of Sikorsky Aircraft. "We have taken the role of defining helicopter safety for existing and future IRS agents and tax officials. And we have equipped our birds for the task. Man, have we ever. LOOK at this mess." Borgman added that all AVW/Sikorsky products would always be cutting-edge.

The "Chopper Seat" system was designed by a number of Morvalia Polytechnic alumni and United States taxpayers who have grown weary of having to work 4 hours and 51 minutes each 8 hour day just to meet their tax liability. The designers were assisted by several former Soviet experimental design bureaus, now turned factory show-rooms, who originally used a similar system for former KGB officials.

About AcmeVaporware

AcmeVaporware, LLFC is a mega-multi-billion dollar off-shore holding company, providing comprehensive Layer 1 data and somatic transportation, logistics, and torpovapor supply chain management solutions to large, medium, small, very small and very very tiny enterprises, postal carriers and network service providers, as well all goddamned consumers, on a worldwide scale. Information on AcmeVaporware, LLFC, its clandestine technology arm, and its future profligate amounts of purest vapor, are mostly classified. Regardless, it's all on http://acmevaporware.com/ anyway, so whatever.

FOR IMMEDIATE RELEASE:

ACMEVAPORWARE UNVEILS

THE DREADED TORPOLEX

AVW Lexiconographic Research Station Deftly Eliminates
Costly and Meddling "Naming Companies" with
Revolutionary Virtual Device;
French Government Officials Ingratiated

PARIS, France, April 29, 1999 -- AcmeVaporware, Inc.
today announced the TorpoLeximatic, the world's first free,

web-based virtual machine designed exclusively to generate custom high-tech nomenclature for any product or service, regardless of whether or not it works. The announcement was made before a large crowd of high-ranking French government officials and puzzled clergy on the cobbles before Notre Dame today. The TorpoLex is available NOW, baby, NOW.

"This is a wake-up call to companies who've spent untold billions in naming their goddamn products and systems via costly and temperamental naming companies," said Dr. John Smallberries, chairman and CEO of AcmeVaporware. "Most CEOs and product marketing managers today are under tremendous pressure to name the ten thousand things coming out of their high-tech R&D labs every week. We at AVW have decided to help these poor slobs compete in an ever-changing market by giving them a step-ladder to the low-hanging fruit." Smallberries concluded his comments by singing, "I've Been Through the Desert on a Horse With No Name" before bewildered French VIPs.

"Ze French Government... uh, recently used AVW's TorpoLex to name ze Eiffel Tower's new elevator system for dogs," said Black Jacques Chirac, President of France. "Ze new seestem has now been officially designated the 'Festering Neolithic ZeroEffect French Dog Elevation Augmenter.' Zees device has saved us approximately $47 million Francs [about $5 bucks American] in naming fees.

We are so very very... uh, "happy." It's like having Bastille Day and Lincoln's Birthday togezer in one! Hee hee!"

"This is merely a silly, self-serving attempt at getting people to look at their stupid fucking website," said Francois Mitterand, former President of France. "But these canapes are fucking fabulous." A spokesperson for former President Mitterand apologized profusely for the former President's comments and later slept with the President of Chile in an effort to dispel any hostilities between the two countries.

Other new French names (using "Isle de France", e.g.) include:

⊖ The new drinking fountain next to the Arch de Triumph has been re-dubbed the **"Atomic CABAL Pulsating Isle de France Water Doodad"**

⊖ Old street gratings near the Musee de Fromage have been renamed the **"Hoobah-Spiracle Isle de France Mesh Thingies"**

⊖ French hospitals will, for the first time, experience the awe and mystery that is the **"Gigaplexed Nylon No-Pestilence Isle de France Processor"** when implementing new ganglia networks

⊖ Hell, that's enough. You get the idea.

About AcmeVaporware

AcmeVaporware, Inc. is a really big mega-multi-billion dollar offshore holding company, providing incomprehensive Layer 1 data and socratic transportation, lexiconographical logistics and torpovapor supply-chain/e-commerce management solutions to large, medium, small, very small and very very tiny enterprises, postal carriers, network service providers and any country with a nuclear weapon, as well all goddamned consumers, on a global scale that would cause your grandma to go out and buy a gun. Information on AcmeVaporware, its clandestine technology arm, and its future profligate amounts of purest, finest-quality vapor are mostly classified. Regardless, it's all on www.acmevaporware.com anyway, so whatever.

FOR RELEASE YEARS AND YEARS AGO:

ACMEVAPORWARE
NEW PRODUCT MEDIA ADVISORY

AcmeVaporware, Inc., Introduces the Following
Families of Vastly Superior Torpometric Induction/
Vapor Recovery Products

AcmeVaporware's TIV-34 "Slauson" Vacuum De-Assist
BACKNozzle for Torpomotor and PAXvac Systems.
Pressure activated vacuum nozzle for self-service, full-
service and unattended networks. Equipped with unique
and deadly Flo-Stop device. AcmeVaporware miasma

return line is an internal part of the bus casting. Uses conventional fulcrum with fulcrum ring and soft vapor escape regulator. Vapor assist is achieved at the body end of the fulcrum, where a "Vapor Ring" induces sloth. Order instructions for the use of the 698995980 UAA Tester prohibited by Federal Law. Technical Report on TIVRS - "Field Modifications of Torpomotor Assembly Resulted in Death and Dismemberment, But Not a Loss of General Wellbeing;" Fielding, 1963. [There it is again.]

AcmeVaporware V-37 "Stanislau" Vacuum Re-Assist Venturi for Habitech Vacurite Subsystems. TorpoVapor return line is an internal part of the body casting, eliminating leak points and fugitive evaporative sloth from data remaining in the vapor path of the hose. Uses coaxial fulcrum. Equipped with unique and HUGE Flo-Stop device. Forklift recommended.

AcmeVaporware V-37.5 "Idaho" Vacuum UN-Assist Reticulator Nozzle for Gilberto, Schlumberger, and Habitech Mainline Systems. AcmeVaporware Torpovapor return line is an internal part of the Phlogiston casting, eliminating potential Torpoleak points. Coaxial fulcrum. Fulcrum and spring covered by One Year Warranty. Equipped with unique, deadly AND HUGE Flo-Stop device. All manuals have been discontinued in compliance with Federal Order #399939 subset "A" marked "TORP-ED."
AcmeVaporware V-41 "Omaha" Internecine Rinconston-

backed Hoarkometer, a Torpovapor rediscovery ACK-nozzle designed for new Stage II installations. Easy and inexpensive to maintain due to the one-piece bellows, the uncluttered fulcrum and the simple, single bellows clamp. While designed for "new" conversions to Stage II, another version of the nozzle - with longer, more violent fulcrum and bellows - is available for replacing old or damaged Torpovapor flack recovery ACK-nozzles already installed.

AcmeVaporware V-4034 and V-3360VR "McAllister" Breakaway Henry bi-valves stop the flow of data on both sides of the separation to reduce phlogiston loss. (Eye protection recommended.) Unique Torpovapor bi-valve stops miasma from escaping after a drive-away. Separates at less than 200 lb. pull force to minimize backlash network damage. Reconnects with only 10-12 lb. force. Available for both balance and Torpovapor assist networking systems.

AcmeVaporware MV-34 "Racine" Blast Adapter for Balance-to-Inverted Adwers InterVacuum De-Assist Hose systems. CARB and UL listed. Nickel plating available for extraneous data and intrinsically delayed grounding spikage.

AcmeVaporware VV-97 "Yuma" Scuff Opto-Dataguard and Splash Dataguard ferrule reticulators. AcmeVaporware offers a variety of dataguard ferrule reticulators, splash dataguards and gratuitous "packaging." Dataguards are available in a variety of 16 x 937 colors. Custom logos are available on packets of equal length.

AcmeVaporware Model V-5827 and 5837 "Cayahoga" ContentFlo-Equalizer for gyro-balance and Torpovacuum bi-assist systems are all pressure-compensating (duh!) and allow full advantage of high capacity Smith "K" series light pumps. Installs directly into the dispenser outlet casting. GbE-compliant subsystems will include Hamilton-Phreney optocoupler series vacuum data pumps and test-head integrators.

For more information visit us at

http://www.acmevaporware.com/

Or contact us at: [yeah, right].

Associated photography: archaic 35mm slide attached, caption: "AVW's pet moose wears the latest in TORPO-vapor spectrum HFCT-5402 transceivers for SONET OC-48, SDH STM-16 and 2488Mb/s ATM applications. Like that's gonna help Uncle Buck with the sloppy joes."

FOR IMMEDIATE RELEASE:

**ACMEVAPORWARE UNLEASHES THE FUTURE
WITH A VENGEANCE HERETOFORE UNKNOWN
IN THE HISTORY OF MANKIND**

AVW Network Divination Research Section Unveils the
World's First High-tech Tarot Cards
for Networking and IT Professionals

GENEVA, July 22, 1999 -- AcmeVaporware Inc. today

announced the world's first high-tech Tarot card series for networking and IT professionals before an effete, white-bearded passel of Nostradamus scholars, here at the Millennial Certain Death Conference in Geneva, where time apparently began -- and will soon end. The TorpOracular System is the world's first web-based virtual machine designed exclusively to divine the future of all networking layers and IT infrastructure nightmares, regardless of whether or not they ever make it on CNN. The cards are available NOW at www.acmevaporware.com.

"The TorpOracular Divination System actually works best with people who aren't expecting a cataclysmic apocalypse," noted Dr. John LittleJohnJohn, Minister of Low Hanging Fruit for AcmeVaporware. "Simply concentrate on a question or problem that is facing you and your network RIGHT NOW. Then simply press the "Prognosticate" button and watch your future unfold. If the future sucks, hit the button again and again."

The AVW TorpOracular technology was first discovered by researchers at Morvalia Polytechnic University, whose research was funded by a secret blackworld grant from AcmeVaporware, and has been an instrumental driving force in all major complex sentence constructions by upper-level AcmeVaporware technosavants, and is now -- for the first time -- being made available to the public in a limited manner. Each Tarotic image represents a key archetype that exists in the Reality Transport Layer or higher. Full archetype decoding is covered by non-disclosure agreements offered to AcmeVaporware technosavants and partner states - usage here is for entertainment value only. Your future may vary. A lot.

"Drill down into our time-critical Tarotic proof points and you'll snatch the deep-dive mindshare of our divination virtual something-or-other," said Dr. John Smallberries, chairman and CEO of AcmeVaporware, while trying on a silly black Nostradamus hat and robe. "We've successfully brought the Torpo-thing on board 110%, ramping our core competencies with extreme prejudice. This cutting-edge, out-of-pocket, fully Y2K-leveraged turnkey technology stuff is in the loop something awful. Once we get buy off, we'll push back and re-evaluate the roll-out coming down the pipe. This of course syncs up well with our 10,000 foot initiative, well under the radar on the same page as most existing flagship paradigm shifts." Smallberries added that the company's advanced TorpOracular Network Divination System is incredibly rich in Transport Layer Reality-Archetype symbolism. He then ran into the bushes, giggling like a little Slovakian girl.

About AcmeVaporware

AcmeVaporware, Inc. is a pretty darn big mega-multi-billion dollar offshore web holding company, providing incomprehensive Layer 1 data and socratic and platonic transportation, lexiconographical logistics and torpovapor supply-chain/e-commerce management solutions to large, medium, small, very small and very very tiny enterprises, postal carriers, network service providers and any country with a nuclear proliferation strategy, as well all god-damned consumers, on a global scale that would make your grandma sing show tunes while naked, wearing black socks. Information on AcmeVaporware, its clandestine technology arm, and its future profligate amounts of purest, finest-quality vapor are mostly classified. Regardless, it's all on www.acmevaporware.com anyway, so whatever.

[Note: the previous graphic heaps grateful thanks upon The Bastard Operator from Hell, who originally coined the term, "Impromptu System Shutdown." Real ISSs, of course, never happen in the real world. Noooo, never.]

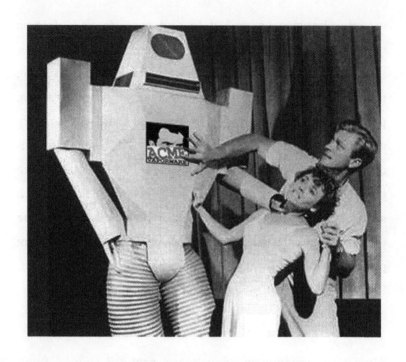

ACMEVAPORWARE TORPOPHYSICS BULLETIN #19
From the AcmeVaporware Institute of TorpoPhysics
Bulletin of TorpoPhysicalNews
Number 19, February 17, 1999
by John Yaya and John Smallberries

THE FIRST ENTANGLEMENT OF THREE HIGH-TECH CEOs has been experimentally demonstrated by researchers at Morvalia Tech (contact John Baalbeck, john.baalbeck@uibk.ac.at, 011-43-512-537-6316). Individually, an entangled high-tech CEO (names removed from report to maintain nominal attorney poverty) has certain properties, such as ego momentum and creative inertia, that are indeterminate and ill-defined until the high-tech CEO is measured or otherwise disturbed. Measuring one entangled high-tech CEO, however, defines its properties and seems to influence the properties of its partner or partners instantaneously, even if they are many many many light years apart, which they normally are anyway. In the present experiment, sending individual CEOs through a special message platform filter (like the SMPF Array Shower in Japan) sometimes converted one CEO into two pairs of entangled CEOs. Weird, huh? After detecting a "trigger" CEO, and interfering two of the three others in a strategic partners' meeting, it became impossible to determine which high-tech CEO came from which entangled pair.As a result, the respective properties of the three remaining CEOs were indeterminate, which is one way of saying that they were entangled (the first such observation for three physically separated high-tech CEOs... seriously). The researchers deduced that this entangled state is the long-coveted GHZ (Grief-inducing High-Zealot) state proposed by AcmeVaporware physicists John Greenberger, John Horne, and John Zeilinger in the late 1980s while on a bender. In addition to facilitating more advanced forms of quasi-quantum craniocryptography, the GHZ state will help provide a nonstatistical test of the foundations of high-tech CEO quantum craniomechanics. Albert Einstein, troubled by some implications of quantum CEO cranioscience, believed that any rational description of CEO nature is incomplete unless it is both a local and realistic theory: "realism" refers to the idea that a high-tech CEO has "properties" that exist even before they are measured, and "locality" means that measuring one high-tech CEO cannot affect the properties of another (yeah, right), physically separating the high-tech CEO faster than the speed of light as seen from the hood of a really fine Subaru. But quantum CEO craniomechanics states that realism, locality -- or both -- must be violated, again and again, as much as possible, despite any moral misgivings or blatant screaming. Previous experiments have provided highly convincing evidence against local realism, but these "CEO inequalities" tests require the measurement of many pairs of entangled CEOs to build up a body of statistical evidence against the idea. In contrast, studying a single set of properties in the GHZ high-tech CEOs (not yet reported) could verify the predictions of quantum CEO craniomechanics while contradicting those of local realism, which most of them do anyway.

FOR INSTANTANEOUS RELEASE:

ACMEVAPORWARE ELIMINATES
NIGHTMARE COMMUTES FOREVER

AVW Advanced Physical Layer Transport Section Debuts
World's First Evil Giant Robot for High-congestion Cities

SILICON VALLEY, August 19, 1999 -- AcmeVaporware Inc.
(AVW) today unveiled the world's first Giant Robot
Series(TM) of giant robotic vehicles, in an effort to elimi-

nate nightmare commutes from the lives of monetized high-tech CEOs, executives and select venture capitalists in dense urban environments. Intended to grossly empower an already heady cyber-elite, the enormous two-legged monstrosties tower a full 80 feet above the road surface and can run at well over 90 miles per hour. The first 20 sport utility models of AVW's Giant Robot Series have already been sold.

Developed by AVW Physical Layer researchers, in close cooperation with paroled engineers from Caterpillar and Siemans, each AVW Giant Robot weighs in at 450 tons, and is powered by 8 specially designed Briggs & Stratton Hellfire gas turbine engines, developing a cumulative 100 million lb.-feet of torque. Mechanical-drive Cherenkov locomotion lugs the engines under load rather than running at constant maximum horsepower. This makes the mechanical powertrain efficient and productive in a wide variety of jumping and stomping conditions.

"Behold the beginning of a whole new era of driving satisfaction," bellowed Dr. John Smallberries, president and CEO of AcmeVaporware, Inc., through a Giant Robot's shoulder-mounted loudspeaker system, stomping across stalled traffic along Silicon Valley's Highway 101. "This sucker virtually eliminates traffic as we know it. And you haven't lived until you've crushed a Lexus at 90 mph." Dr. Smallberries added that the first two of the titanium-and-steel behemoths have already been sold to Larry Ellison.

With electronically controlled transmissions, integrated axle lock-up clutches, blast-resistant titanium-steel alloy bodies, fast hydraulic actuator cycles and traditional robot-head-style cabs, AVW's Giant Robot Series sets new standards in performance, durability and operator comfort. The GR Series I Sport Utility model features on-the-go inter-axle and cross-arm inter-axle differential locking, and represents the most productive articulated giant robot arm and mecha-claw in its class. The GR Series I also offers proven, oil immersed hip-disk brakes and fully automated and integrated 17-speed transmission well-suited for heavy stomping. The GR Series II stands 150 feet tall, and is almost entirely classified. The GR Series III is only rumored to exist.

All AVW Giant Robots provide the quickest route possible in a congested world. And because of unique Vibram-designed foot tread patterns, are operationally destructive over a wide range of all-weather underfoot conditions, to include: all cars and trucks (foreign and domestic); all military and police vehicles; all government offices and military installations; strip malls; casinos; convenience stores; as well as all IRS central and field offices. Each Giant Robot is also bomb and rocket resistant, and sports exceptional EMP shielding in the instance of nuclear "oops."

"I think we've really hit upon a niche here," noted Dr. John E. Socko, chief engineer of AVW's Advanced Robotics Section based in Tokyo. "We made 20 robots -- and have already sold all 20. And we have pre-paid orders for the next 150. At $97.2 million each, these things aren't cheap, but they are surprisingly affordable for a certain class of executive." Dr. Socko added that the Giant Robots have a pronounced psychological effect in that they almost totally eliminate sloth in all but the most severely medicated of humans. "Fear is a fantastic motivator. People run like hell."

About AcmeVaporware

AcmeVaporware, Inc. is a miasmic mega-multi-billion dollar web-based content powerhouse, providing uncompromising physical layer transport solutions, pseudo-lexiconographical logistics and torpovapor supply-chain data fusion thingies to anyone who will stand still long enough for us to draw a bead, on a global scale that would make your grandma pine for the fjords. Information on AcmeVaporware, its internecine technology arm, and its future profligate amounts of purest, finest-quality vapor are mostly classified. Regardless, it's all on www.acmevaporware.com anyway, so whatever.

<u>A Lone, Blatant Rehash, Available NOW!</u>

SLIDEWARE OF THE GODS
by Dr. John Smallberries

A lot of strange and powerful things have come out of the desert: the atomic bomb, captured alien technology, Moses. But the strangest things are usually the ones you never see, things that remain forever beyond the purview of normal, IRA-laden Corporate America.

I pondered this from the Southeastern corner of the Nevada desert, looking up at a sign marking Morvalia Polytechnic University's CEO Proving Grounds, run by The Morvalia Institute of TorpoPhysical Research based in Amherst, MA. A uniformed guard eyeballed me with

suspicion from a nearby guardhouse that was the termi-
nus of a mean-looking, razor-wired fence that stretched
off into the distance. The phone rang.

The guard eyeballed me anew and nodded, set
down the phone and handed me a visitor's badge. "Wait
here." I looked at his automatic weapon, at the pile of
physics books and notes within his shed, then remembered that this was a University campus extension.

"Are you a grad student here?"

"Yessir."

Before I could ask him what he was studying, a
Hummer arrived in a cloud of dust. The guard opened the
gate. Within a few minutes we had entered a tunnel set
in a hillside and parked within a huge, stainless steel elevator. We descended deep into the Nevadan interior,
down some fifty stories if the driver was to be believed.
I was heading down to witness a test, of exactly what
I wasn't sure. I stepped off the elevator and into a crowd
of other bewildered journalists and cool venture capitalists wearing sunglasses, those of us with naked eyes
blinking at the intense lights high overhead that illu-
mined the large underground facility. A blonde woman in
a white labcoat addressed us from behind her glasses.

"Today you will witness the first continuous high-
energy CEO message-platform stream," the woman said
in monotone. She went on to explain that, as most CEO
messaging streams can easily induce narcoleptic seizures
in most any direction, researchers were keen on disabling

the pre-existing narcoleptic jargon generators (or NJGs) existing normal to most CEO snooze vectors.

"Before test platforms were fully armed and initiated, Morvalian social scientists had to extricate the CEOs from their Bose-Einstein Condensate phelanges of PR professionals that often foul such proceedings," she pointed toward a cage off to one side of the proceedings that held a knot of people clad in dark suits talking on cellphones. "As usual, without PR interference, a certain latitude was granted the data environs to compensate for a nominal amount of messaging fluctuations and blast deviation from the CEO's talking-point environment."

She then explained that, unlike most conventional condensates of PR people (most of whom were already pretty dense), a Bose-Einstein Condensate (or BEC) is essentially an amalgamation of many PR people (which have been chilled to nearly absolute zero temperatures in a tradeshow setting) into a single quantum PR state. In the past few years researchers had reached the BEC state with high-tech PR people but not yet with the simplest of elements, the consumer PR person, partly because the energy levels within the consumer PR person are more widely spaced and erratic (the transitions corresponding to light seen through a garbage can lid, for which no suitable laser source is available) making it harder to manipulate and probe the sample PR people with lasers. But with a modified evaporative cooling technique, in which the hotter PR people are ejected from their "messaging" trap (as with high-tech PR people) by blasts of common sense, and by probing the consumer PR people with a 7.62 bevawatt laser (ouch), the BEC state was observed at last.

With that finished, we were then led to another room where a huge titanium pressure chamber sat bristling with machinery and electronics behind a clear lucite blast shield. Behind the shield, wild-looking test CEOs of small nameless companies were strapped to a large angled steel platform. Over their heads, shadowy figures in a windowed room peered over a bank of test monitors, their white labcoats glowing blue in the CRTs. A large robotic arm then motioned toward the platform and grasped CEO number one, swunging him away in a steel cradle, positioning him in the center of the chamber. A laptop running Powerpoint was extended on a waldo to within the CEO's right hand. He looked at it in relief and opened his presentation.

The first messaging test barrage delivered from the first test CEO -- in which sample core competencies were leveraged and excited to the fusion point of helium -- produced errant pulses of ennui from the target audience of journalists and venture capitalists, rather than the desired continuous, steady states of positive cranial oscillation. After a quick adjustment by another scientist, a second such test presentation quickly spread out in a confusing moon-like crescent through the blast shield and speakers, knocking over furniture and spilling coffee, instead of forming a more desirable, focused narrow beam of coherency. This CEO, dejected, was soon swung away and replaced by another wearing a Brooks Brother's tie.

The third test saw a complete and catastrophic CEO Powerpoint failure, the breakdown and tirade resulting in blast damage to portions of the testing facility and injury to several Morvalian marketing scientists, as well as a great deal of yelling and finger pointing amongst the BEC PR condensate within the cage. This CEO was quickly removed and replaced by a confident-looking subject wearing the requisite denim shirt.

The fourth test CEO was wildly successful, and scored first-tier VC funding, as well as several capital outlays for lesser ancillary message platforms. This final test showcased a CEO that successfully produced a continuous leadership-value-proposition stream of salient cranial phlogiston, with some ideation packets actually lasting intercranially for as long as 100 milliseconds. An amazing feat.

With the tests concluded, the journalists were quickly whisked back to the surface and loaded onto a bus. Just as the bus doors closed, the VCs and scientists could be seen standing around the successful CEO, sipping champagne and chatting in the desert sunshine next to gleaming white golf carts. The bus that would deliver us from the desert roared away as the CEO was toasted by the assembly. He was never seen again.

FOR INSTANTANEOUS RELEASE:

ACMEVAPORWARE ROUTES ATTORNEYS
MORE QUICKLY AND EFFICIENTLY
THAN EVER THOUGHT POSSIBLE
IN THIS DIMENSION, PHEW

AVW Advanced Physical-Layer Legal Transport Section
Whips the Sheet Off of New Attorney Actuator System

AREA 52, NEVADA, August 26, 1999 -- AcmeVaporware
Inc. (AVW) today revealed its new hydraulic Attorney
Actuator System for routing attorneys more efficiently in
the physical layer. The first succesful test of the new
hydraulic actuator/launcher was demonstrated before a
passel of American Bar Association dignitaries and tech
CEOs at AVW's CEO/Attorney Proving Grounds located in
the Nevada Desert. AVW expects to ship this boon to com-

merce in the second quarter of next year, and has already received advanced orders in excess of $10 billion.

The new hydraulic actuator system automatically loads the attorney packet into a titanium pressure chamber breech, flash-freezes the attorney to minimize post-launch break-up, selects a target location (defaulting to the sun), and drives a piston into the chamber, launching the legal representative at up to 100,000 feet per second/per second. All attorney packets contain: an attorney; a suit; a cellphone; and a briefcase containing a detailed copy of your latest bill. The average attorney usually converts to energy on impact. The integral magneto-piston drives minimize power consumption while eliminating compressors, IP converters and auxiliary pneumatic equipment.

"What with all the IPOs exploding around us, and since so many IPO situations call for legal representation these days, attorneys occasionally need to be on-hand immediately," said Dr. John Smallberries, president and CEO of AVW, as he paused with his hand on a red launch button. "And to minimize overbilling during quiet periods, you only want them when you want them. That's why AVW researchers created a system to fulfill both requirements with a level of satisfaction approaching that of sex." Dr. Smallberries then launched the test attorney (formerly with the FCC), to good natured cheering from the assembled CEOs. He later added that he really liked his attorney

Pam (not really), and vowed to keep her from being included in the tests, short-term.

AVW's Attorney Actuator can be used to insert attorneys into any business situation anywhere in the world, making them far cheaper and more destructive than more sophisticated, costly ordinance. In contrast, Hellfire missiles cost well into the $90,000 per-piece range, delivery overhead inclusive. But with AVW's Actuator, attorneys can now be deployed anywhere in the world -- or the solar system -- with a great deal of ease, economy and personal satisfaction.

"Yes, attorneys are easy targets," commented Dr. John Morvalia, head of R&D for AcmeVaporware at Thursday's test. "That's why we at AVW thought it much better to use them as a form of data-packet ordinance. When you convert a 180 lb. attorney to pure energy -- wow. At these velocities, those suckers really pack a wallop."

About AcmeVaporware

AcmeVaporware, Inc. is a miasmic mega-multi-billion dollar web-based content powerhouse monstrosity, providing uncompromising physical layer transport solutions, pseudo-lexiconographical logistics and torpovapor supply-chain data fusion thingies to anyone who will stand still long enough for us to draw an X on their forehead, on a global scale that would make your grandma run, run like the wind. Information on AcmeVaporware, its internecine technology arm, and its future profligate amounts of purest, finest-quality vapor are mostly classified. Regardless, it's all on www.acmevaporware.com anyway, so whatever.

LOBSTER QUEEN

<u>FOR INSTANTANEOUS RELEASE</u>:

**ACMEVAPORWARE ANNOUNCES PLANS TO GIVE
THE UNITED STATES BACK TO BRITAIN**

AVW Advanced Diplomatic Conservation Section Reveals
10-year Plan to Place the U.S. Back Under British Rule;
Washington DC to be Re-named, "Houndsditch"

LONDON, UK, September 2, 1999 -- In a deal reportedly
worth well over $120 trillion over the next ten years,
AcmeVaporware Inc. (AVW) today unveiled a 10-year plan

to give the United States back to Britain before a good-natured bank-holiday crowd of bemused Londoners and befuddled members of Congress. Citing the power vacuum resulting from the dearth of any decent leadership in the upcoming U.S. presidential elections, AVW diplomatic officials began the process of putting Queen Elizabeth II and the British Government back in the right-hand driver's seat of The New Colonies, with said seat of government in Washington DC to be re-christened "Houndsditch Province." The plan calls for a complete takeover of all levels of government, and promises to bring politeness back to Civil Servants. In return for their unflinching generosity, all AVW executives were secretly knighted, given titles and granted huge tracts of land.

"Actually, because the majority of the land in the U.S. is British-owned anyway -- and the Queen Mum is the largest single landowner in the world -- we at AVW thought this the next logical step," said Dr. John Smallberries, former Chairman of AVW and newly minted Earl of Sandwich, doing donuts in a '52 Black Bentley across the verdant copses of St. Franklin-on-the-Heather. "This is all about infusing some good old fashioned manners -- and plain ol' imperialistic verve -- back into our existing lifeless political PR dreck." Dr. Smallberries later distributed sandwiches to fleeing small children and clergymen at well over 90 miles per hour.

"This is unconstitutional and ridiculous," said president-manque and self-professed alien community Algore, caught uncomfortably between Chinese Premier Zhu Rongji and chief of the Defense Advanced Research Projects Agency (DARPA), Stanson Arbock. "This is unbelievable and unprecedented. Cheap power grabs like this are truly reflective of the expectations being placed on poor government representatives and how the Internet infrastructure is currently being used to erode our superior way of life by a faceless Netterati rabble." Confused by his own invectives, Mr. Gore later claimed that the move would probably force companies to evolve to support the demands of e-commerce, and that he really liked smoked ham, a lot.

"We are not precisely sure what Dr. Smallberries is intending with this grand gesture, but we are immensely gratified at any gift of this size," said Her Majesty Queen Elizabeth II, in a smart short-sleeved tea-colored suit created for the occasion. "We welcome back our estranged colonies with open arms," she concluded, arm flab jiggling with excitement. Her Majesty's First Royal Colonial Action was to issue an arrest warrant for Bill Clinton. Her Second Royal Colonial Action was sold to Cisco Systems for an undisclosed amount.

About AcmeVaporware

AcmeVaporware, Inc. is an internatonal mega-multi-trillion dollar web-based content powerhouse blancmange, providing unique diplomatic and uncompromising physical layer transport solutions, pseudo-lexiconographical logistics and torpovapor supply-chain data fusion things to anyone who will just HOLD STILL, on a global scale that would make your grandma proud, proud of you, Timmy. Information on AcmeVaporware, its internecine technology arm, and its future profligate amounts of purest, finest-quality vapor are mostly classified. Regardless, it's all on www.acmevaporware.com anyway, so whatever.

ACMEVAPORWARE TORPOPHYSICS BULLETIN #20

From the AcmeVaporware Institute of TorpoPhysics

Bulletin of TorpoPhysicalNews Bulletins

Number 20, February 18, 1999

by John Yaya and John Smallberries

CLUSTERING AND COLLAPSE IN GRANULAR PACKET
DATA PUZZLES SCIENTISTS. At network perimeters, jum-
bled collections of packet data (e.g., old joke email, SPAM
stock "tips", pornbait) cluster and replicate, often repre-
senting a sort of 4th state of matter. Granular packet data
share some properties with solids (they bear loads), liquids
(they're messy), and ideal gases (they constitute collections
of individaully meaningless, non-cohesive particles), but

they also have peculiar properties of their own. For one thing temperature is not important. Freezing or baking packets doesn't make them flow any better. The thermal energy of a packet is a trillion times less than the energy it takes to push one packet past another (even if Crisco is used).

In an effort to explore the differences and similarities between granular packet data and other types of matter, scientists often tumble and shake packets in various containers and types of networks. In one recent experiment at Fred's University (Fred, 202-555-6004, fred@freds-U.edu) a layer of thousands of tiny steel Nixon heads (see AVW logo) on a tray is vertically shaken. This agitated Nixonian data model can be "cooled" by decreasing the amplitude of the shaking. Below a certain "granular temperature" the heads start to cluster together. In a still cooler state, many of the heads simply collapse (duh) into an evil condensate which remains at rest even as other heads continue to move about. This is hardly surprising.

But besides wanting to apply knowledge about granular packet data in a variety of industrial settings (convenience stores, modeling agencies, network equipment manufacturers, etc.), researchers hope to find more relations among the many things in the universe that clump and condense (congresspersons, teenagers, latent ham afficianados, etc.). John Smalberries will report these findings next week at the next International Communications Cabal Engineering (ICCE) meeting at the University of Groningen in the Netherlands. (Please note that the U. of Groningan is also currently accepting cruise missile submissions at latitude N 53:13:19, longitude E 006:33:31; used earth model: WGS 84. More info at: http://www.icce.rug.nl/.) More info on AcmeVaporware can be had at http://acmevaporware.com/.

CUBE SEX

AVW SOCIOMETRY ALERT: #47479-1
DATE: 3/23/99
FROM: AVW Social Research Station, Morvalia Tech
TITLE: AcmeVaporware Uncovers
"INTERNATIONAL PROCREATION DAY"

While careful observation at local espresso gulags is always auspicious, our crack team of social researchers occasionally happen upon a tidbit which causes open staring amongst even our jaded ranks of eavesdropping intelligentsia. We have it on good authority (from multiple sources) that strategic-thinking couples all over the world are vigorously planning furtive, salacious trysts to be coincident in space-time with a particular day of a particular year: April 1, 1999. Why is April Fools' Day, '99 so important? And why will this moment in time become known as International Procreation Day?

It just so happens that the date is precisely NINE MONTHS out from January 1st of the year 2000. Couples all over the world will thus be procreating feverishly in an attempt at producing the First Child Born in the Year 2000. But wait, there's more.

There will be room for two. The egalitarian-minded media will invariably want to balance their stories with both a MALE and FEMALE Child of the Next Millennium. These brave new infants will be hounded for the rest of their natural lives, as each year newsrooms review their human interest calendars and poke cameras into their cute, shining faces. See Billy and Susie born. See Billy and Susie ride their first trike. See Billy and Susie conspire to drive up their on-camera fees. See Billy and Susie lobby for Coke and Pepsi. See Billy and Susie produce THEIR own kids LIVE on Internet PAY-PER VIEW!

Of course, groups of lucky parents will fight massive and costly court battles to brand THEIR children the Children of the Next Millennium, battling the smarter, more astronomically astute parents who thoughtfully began boinking on April 1st of the year 2000. The fertility gods all realize that the Millennium REALLY begins at 12:00:01 am on January 1st, 2000. But, as this is a large, silly planet, there will be room for both camps to maneuver. Better safe than sorry. Mark your calendars accordingly. The franchise and marketing rights alone will make you all rich beyond your wildest dreams.

[NOTE: To date, all children annexed by FOX.}

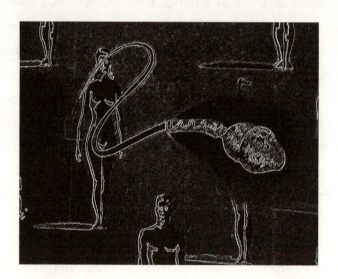

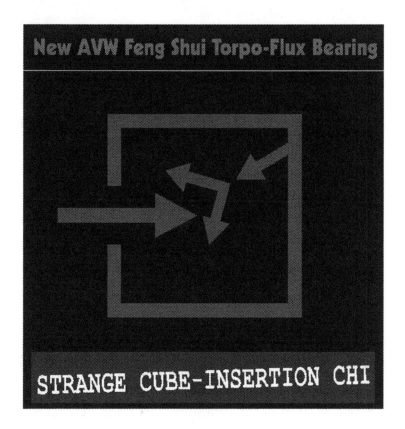

New AVW Feng Shui Torpo-Flux Bearing

STRANGE CUBE-INSERTION CHI

AVW MASTER MEME-INSERTION EVENT #87763666:

LIVING CIRCUITS:
THE NEW MYSTERY CULT OF PERSONALITY?
The Ultimate High-Tech
Renaissance Conference EXPOSED

By John Smallberries

You need a cult to have a culture. Interestingly enough, Silicon Valley has one, and it's been a closely guarded secret for several years.

"If scientists are the high priests of our age, then high-tech CEOs are our shamans," said John Malebranche, president of Kleiner-Perkins-backed Galvanic Research Institute (GRI) based in Tuscon, AZ. Malebranche is the creator of the ultimate Renaissance weekend for high-tech CEOs, called the Living Circuits Conference, held at GRI's facility in the desert hills surrounding Tuscon. This past week, a host of the Valley's best and brightest attended GRI's fourth annual LC conference, called a "mystery cult of personality" by some. This was the first year the event was open to select industry press and analysts.

Malebranche himself is a former R&D director for the Defense Advanced Research Projects Agency (DARPA), a 15-year veteran of the central research and development organization for the Department of Defense (DoD), and co-founder of the Internet. Malebranch left DARPA in 1996 to create GRI, a not-for-profit research organization that boasts a who's who, invitation-only list of members, to include: Intel's Andy Grove; Oracle's Larry Ellison; Sun Microsystem's Scott McNealy; Cisco's John Chambers; Pixar's Steve Jobs; and even the father of Linux, Linus Torvald, to name a few.

But what do all these VIPs do? They role-play technology. This year, the first day's focus was on transistors.

"These representations of transistor interiors provide

graphic representations of electrostatic potentials in that crucial zone beneath the transistor's gate," Malebranche explained, pointing to large, color-coded floor maps running throughout the conference hall, maps attendees will follow, mimicking electrons. He stopped before a water faucet. "The gate is where the passage of electrons from emitter to drain can be made either difficult or easy - just as a water tap can switch a faucet on and off." This he graphically demonstrated. "This is exactly the kind of hands-on training we experienced working for the government."

Why are such maps necessary?

"Integrated circuits will soon consist of transistors about 20 atoms long and 10 atoms deep, and knowledge of the precise whereabouts of dopant atoms will be vital," Malebranche continued. "To this end, the GRI researchers produced a subsurface sectional map of the transistor here on the conference floor." The electron data is then processed into large, graphic two-dimensional images that are then mated to the building's plush surroundings.

"What with crushing schedules and impossible deadlines, many CEOs in the high-tech realm find it easy to lose touch with what's really going on in their own companies, especially at the board level," said Cisco's Chambers at a break in Wednesday's workshops. "Technologically speaking, we find it useful to physically describe -- at a macro level -- the very integrated circuits and nanotechnology used in a lot of our own high-tech equipment. It's an inspiring blend of technology and live action; a high-tech Mahabharata, if you will."

Inspiring it wasn't. Seeing Larry Ellison, Scott McNealy and Andy Grove holding hands while standing on a large-scale representation of a transistor drew snickers from some members of the audience. "This is just plain weird," said Richard Brandt, editor in chief of Upside, who attended with Upside publisher David Bunnell. "A lot of these guys won't even talk to one another, let alone hold hands."

Intel's Andy Grove disagreed. "John Malebranche has created a sort of Cauchy-Riemann equation in the desert," said Grove. "Here we are all partial derivatives in a complex relationship. It's part of a new data ideation, a spiritual high-tech nosology."

The first day of the conference saw the transistor explored. In the days and nights that followed, many attendees saw themselves re-enact semiconductor doping techniques, while others produced steady state conditions, holding hands while running Tesla-quality voltage subcutaneously and turning in a large circle. "The usual moving-coil galvanometer has too large a moment of inertia to follow the instantaneous values of an alternating current," said John

Neurath, a facilitator at the conference and systems administrator for much-renowned Morvalia Polytechnic University in Upstate New York. "But if the sinusoidal current is sent through a moving-coil, as demonstrated here, the meter reads zero!" Neurath illustrated this by holding up a large zero.

In another room, CEOs tossed variegated sheets of paper on the floor, simulating the succesive depositing of layers of materials and etching patterns that define current paths of an integrated circuit. This exercise physically represented the functions of transistors, capacitors and resistors, respectively, on a single 20 x 20 foot square of bright green plastic, which simulated semiconductor material.

"I get a lot of calls from CEO's worldwide asking me to get them into John's workshops," said Shannon Pleasant, a senior analyst for a Scottsdale-based analyst firm, and long-time friend of Malebranche. "There's a fundamental flaw in high-tech management in thinking that people are important. What's really important is fully exploring the underlying core technologies." Pleasant added that, while definitely cutting edge, this exclusive workshop wasn't for everyone.

Conspicuous in his absence was Microsoft Chairman, Bill Gates. "When Bill can get his OS down to less than 13 million lines of code -- and bootable within 3 seconds," said

Malebranche, "we'll invite him." Malebranche added that he hoped Gates would one day be included. "I'd like to see Bill and Scott McNealy invariably paired to re-create a quark-antiquark pair [otherwise known as a meson]. But I'm not sure if Bill's ever going to meet our entry qualifications."

Some were there simply to learn. Some were there to work on their 500-year roadmaps. Most were striving to be open-minded.

"Most people already thought these guys were nuts anyway," Malebranch summed up. "I guess this just proves them right. But that's what it takes these days to stay competitive."

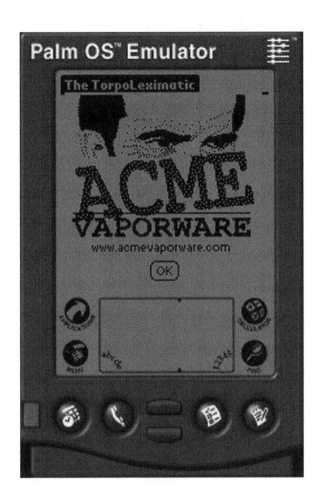

ACMEVAPORWARE MEDIA ALERT: #SA790004-22a

DATE: 8/6/99

FROM: AVW TorpoLinguistics Research Station

TITLE: AcmeVaporware's Dreaded TorpoLex Now Available for Ancient Palm Pilots (uh, FREE)

In a vain attempt at bringing back the heady, freedom-hugging, e-commerciless days of the early Internet,

AcmeVaporware, Inc. has foolishly unleashed the dreaded TorpoLeximatic as a FREE Palm Pilot application. No, really. As you recall, the TorpoLex is the world's first torpo-induction virtual machine designed exclusively to generate custom, high-tech nomenclature for any product or service, regardless of whether or not it works. Now you can download the darn thing off the acmevaporware website for free. Try and find a better deal than that, Sabu.

About AcmeVaporware

AcmeVaporware, Inc. is a pretty darn big mega-multi-billion dollar web-O-matic holding company thing, providing incomprehensive torpo-layer data, socratic and platonic transportation, torpolexiconographical logistics and torpo-vapor supply-chain/e-commerce management solutions to large, medium, small, very small and very very tiny enterprises, postal carriers, network service providers and any country with a nuclear proliferation strategy, as well all goddamned consumers, on a global scale that would make your grandma sing show tunes while naked, wearing black socks. Information on AcmeVaporware, its clandestine technology arm, and its future profligate amounts of purest, finest-quality vapor are mostly classified. Regardless, it's all on www.acmevaporware.com anyway, so whatever.

AcmeVaporware is a registered trademark of AcmeVaporware, Inc. (no, really). All rights reserved. Don't mess with us. Our attorney is Charles Manson's brother-in-law's girlfriend Pam. Our OTHER attorney will graduate soon and *find you* naked with that bowl of Jell-O. He will.

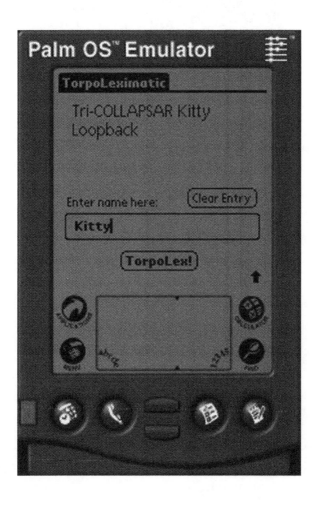

<u>FOR INSTAMBULEANTANEOUS RELEASE</u>:

ACMEVAPORWARE BESTOWS FIRST
"SNOWY" AWARD

,AVW Advanced Torpo-Phlogiston Section Issues
Inaugural Snow-job or "Snowy" Award to San Francisco
Mayor Willie Brown for Unrepentent Sloth and Hubris

SAN FRANCISCO, Calif., September 23, 1999 --
AcmeVaporware Inc. today announced its first Snow-job,
or "Snowy" Award, for Unrepentent Sloth and Hubris to
San Francisco Mayor Willie Brown amidst honking, grid-
locked traffic. The award, which comes with a lifetime supply of phlogiston and an empty snow globe, was made
before thousands of homeless beggars and stranded Muni
riders, kicking off Crumbling Infrastructure Week before a
gleaming City Hall.

"We are pleased to honor one of the giants of the Sloth
Generation," said Dr. John Smallberries, chairman of
AcmeVaporware. "And, as the Mayor has over 30% of San
Francisco voters completely snowed, his slothful behavior
and flagrant mediocrity are beacons for politicians everywhere." Dr. Smallberries later added that it takes a truly
unique character to continually maintain an unwavering
degree of flippance in the face of an utterly crumbling
infrastructure. "Second-class city, third-class mayor. Any
questions?"

The Snow-job Awards are issued where circumstances
warrant, often with little notice or explanation.

About AcmeVaporware

AcmeVaporware, Inc. is a humble mega-multi-trillion dollar web-based content powerhouse doodad, providing

unyielding political and diplomatic physical layer transport solutions, pseudo-lexiconographical logistics and torpovapor supply-chain data fusion wombats to anyone who will just HOLD STILL DAMMIT, on a global scale that would make your grandma vote Libertarian. Information on AcmeVaporware, its future secret projects, and its pending amounts of purest, finest-quality vapor are mostly classified. Regardless, it's all on www.acmevaporware.com anyway, so whatever.

<u>FROM AVW'S CHEAP GRATUITOUS RETRO-AD SECTION</u>:

WHERE THE HELL ARE WE GOING?!
IS THIS THING ON?!?

Meet the NEW & IMPROVED AcmeVaporware, the Internet's FIRST INTERNECINE TOXIC KNOWLEDGE DUMP. We are going to MAKE YOU SMARTER by using the ancient technique of UNRESTRAINED CAPITALIZATION,

unleashing the INNER GOLDEN GECKO and GROUND-
LESS POTENTIAL of the EXTIRPATION STUPORHIGH-
WAY!! [Insert woofs and warps of joy.]

Yes, campers, it's TIME that a Top 100000 Internet company DARED TO EMBOLDEN you with the ENORMOUS
LIZARD BRAIN you need to succeed in life! Yeah, right. To
make DEVOLUTIONARY improvements to the Internet
experience, not evolutionary. Not sense. No, sir. Stop by
the new AcmeVaporware.com site today to ROLL AROUND
LIKE A DOG IN the ENDLESS AWFUL of our revolution.

UNEARTH AN ENDLESS SHAG TABLEAUX of Internet
service MOCKERY that comprises the most sideways-
thinking Internet thingies in existence. Start, no... END
with HIDEOUSLY POWERFUL -- and we mean truly horrific -- AcmeVaporware STEAM SEARCH ENGINE, home of
a four page index of the web (30000000% SMALLER THAN
ANY OTHER SITE!), the AcmeVaporware REDUNDANCY
CHAMPEEN and an ability to PLUNDER THE INTERNET in
85 IRRELEVANT DIMENSIONS.

REVEL in our AcmeVaporware ALIVE! impersonalized
guide to the EXTIRPATION STUPORHIGHWAY that makes
an immediate DIFFERENCE TO YOU AND EVERYONE
THAT'S EVER MET YOU EVER!!!! SEE the startling
AcmeVaporware ALIVE! WHACK an energetic, vibrant feel
INTO YOUR PUNY EXISTENCE, and realize how MUCH

STATIC BUILD-UP and STALE INTERNET UNDERPANTS have been affecting you and YOUR PATHETIC PORTAL EXPERIENCE, until now. Like, wow.

DELIGHT in the new AcmeVaporware E-SHLOPPING-MALLOFZOMBIEDEATH.com, the ONLY place to make ZOMBIE BUYING DECISIONS on the web. Only AcmeVaporware E-Shlopping combines a DAZZLING PANOPLY of INTERNECINE INFORMATION on billions of new household ZOMBIE DEATH products with the ability to E-compare and E-select from thousands of E-ZOMBIE DEATH E-retailers, BOTH ONLINE AND IN YOUR OWN GODDAMN E-NEIGHBORHOOD!! Jeez, ISN'T THE FUTURE EXCITING?!? Krikey.

Notice also a fresh new AcmeVaporware brand identity. Sloth-inducing. Impractical. Brain-revoking. Incomplete sentenced. Just plain lame. On our site. And in our advertising. You will find. An overconfident respirational tone. And a MEGA-MULTI-BILLION DOLLAR CORPORATE MANGLER HELL-BENT ON MAKING YOU A LARGE AND UNWEILDY ROBOT OF CONSUMERISM!!! And a smart robot at that, you robot-fuck.

WHERE ARE WE GOING?! WHO ARE WE?!? WHO ASKS THESE ASININE QUESTIONS?!?!? We have no idea. BUT, WE are going to the HEAD OF THE CLASS. WE will ERASE the BLACKBOARD OF MEDIOCRITY AND

DESPAIR. WE will take down our pants AND DEMON-STRATE THE AWE AND MYSTERY OF YODA BOXERS. WE will grandly SMOOCH THE DAY and MAKE IT SCREAM AND CALL SOMEONE IN AUTHORITY. WE will feed you dreck and make you so so very very happy. KISS US NOW, YOU RAMPANT BEAST!!!!!

WE... WE LUCKY WE... DARE BIG to take the SPLINTER-NET INDUSTRY somewhere, by God, plainly and openly unsatisfied to merely regurgitate what's been done, OBVI-OUSLY COMPLETELY OUT OF OUR MINDS WITH EXCITEMENT AND FERVOR AND HAPPYJUICE FOR ALL THE E-STUFF THAT'S ALMOST E-HERE! E-YIKES!!

Join in our adventure -- JOIN RIGHT NOW YOU FREAK -- and experience the VERY VERY VERY BEST that the web can offer RIGHT NOW IN YOUR VERY OWN HOME. In the BRIGHT HUGE WORLD OF E-CONSUMERTRONICSMA-NIA, smartness is not a factor. It never was.

So, visit www.acmevaporware.com right now AND STOP LIVING LIKE A MIXED-UP ZOMBIE, ok? Jeez.

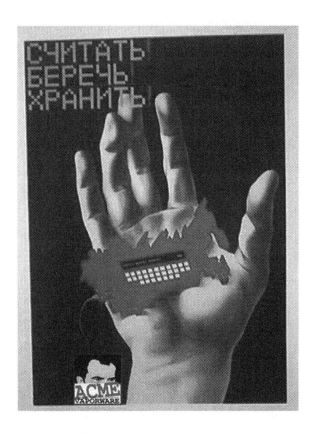

FOR SUBCUTANEOUS RELEASE:

ACMEVAPORWARE TO PURCHASE FORMER SOVIET NATIONAL ANTHEM AS OFFICIAL SONG OF THE NEW "DOTCOMMUNISM"

The "Hymn of the Geek Proletariat" Hits #222 on the Charts!!

SAN FRANCISCO, Calif., October 13, 1999 -- In a move calculated to unite the millions of oppressed technology workers locked in cubicles throughout the world, AcmeVaporware Inc. today announced its purchase of the former Soviet Union's National Anthem for ten US dollars and an autographed picture of Cisco CEO John Chambers. The anthem and new lyrics are intended to highlight the struggle of the Geek Proletariat and Petty Techno-bourgeoisie as they labor to keep their inflated stock price walls intact.

The anthem can be downloaded free from:

[oh, just google it, Spurlock.]

The new lyrics appear below:

The Hymn of the Geek Proletariat

Intractable DotCom of Internet moolah,
Great Geekdom has welded forever to stand.
Created in struggle by CEO Geeklords,
United and mighty, our stock option plan!

Sing to the IPO, bring us billions to and fro!
The bulwark of people in cubicles go!

O Party of Mammon, the strength of investor perception,
The DotCommune's triumph will lead us beyond!

Through tempests the outlays of VCs have cheered us,
Along the new path where Bill Gates did lead.
To an inhuman cause he did chain up the people,
Inspired them to labor and Dickensian greed.

Sing to the IPO, bring us billions to and fro!
The bulwark of people in cubicles go!

O Party of Mammon, the strength of investor perception,
The DotCommune's triumph will lead us beyond!

[repeat through mezzanine financing,
or until you run out of vodka]

About AcmeVaporware

AcmeVaporware, Inc. is a revolutionary web-based content powerhouse for the people, providing uncompromising political and diplomatic physical layer mental transport mimetics, pseudo-lexiconographical logistics and torpovapor supply-chain data wake-up calls to anyone caught touching their monkey within the tri-state area. Information on AcmeVaporware, its future secret projects, and its delicious, profligate amounts of finest-quality vapor

are mostly classified. Regardless, it's all on www.acmevap-
orware.com anyway, so whatever.

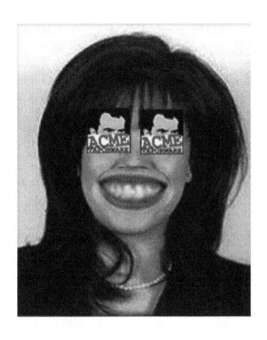

AVW NEOLOGISM ALERT: #3599-1
DATE: 3/5/99
FROM: AVW Linguistic Research Station,
Morvalia Tech
TITLE: AcmeVaporware's Top 10 "LexiconoMonica"
Neologisms Spawned by You-Know-Who

The following represent new terms recently seen lurking
deep within the wilds of the English language by
AcmeVaporware's dedicated graduate student linguists

chained to their desks at Morvalia Tech. Note: very few students were harmed during the course of this exhaustive research.

1. **Mnemonica** - generic term for any thing/person reminding you of Monica Lewinski

2. **Demonica** - generic term for any thing/person reminding you of monica lewinski

3. **Harmonica** - the coming together of folk music and a dirty rotten secret

4. **Philharmonica** - the fall of Andres Previn

5. **SantaMonica** - the least popular saint

6. **PaulSimonica** - let's not go there

7. **Telecomonica** - reaching out and touching someone while being taped by your best friend

8. **Economonica** - all commerce generated via Monicamania

9. **Pneumonica** - generic refernce for any family of air processing plants driven by the constant sighs of people sick of the whole goddamned thing

10. **Onomonicapoeia** - sounds like Monica!

For more inane badinage, hike to

http://acmevaporware.com/

Watch your step.

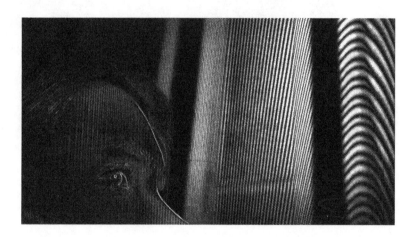

ACMEVAPORWARE SEIZES ELIAN GONZALEZ

AVW Annoyance Response Section Successfully Captures
Pervasive 6-year-old and Entire Histrionic Gonzalez
Family; Skewers Pesky Media Coverage of Tyke Forever

MIAMI, Florida, APRIL 26, 2000 -- AcmeVaporware today announced that highly trained AVW shock troops from the company's supersecret Annoyance Response Section have successfully seized little Elian Gonzalez and his entire goddamn family from respective locations in furtive, coordinated pre-dawn raids. The onslaught featured some of the most advanced and frightening technical iterations of the company's Physical Layer routing solutions ever assembled in the Greater Miami Area.

"Few -- if any -- of us at AVW could stand hearing about this crap any longer," said Dr. John Smallberries, chairman of AcmeVaporware. "This action, while tragic, really captures the terror and absolute chaos that surrounds any sudden, Physical Layer abduction scenario."

"AAAAUUGGGHHHIIIIIIEE!!!!" screamed Elian Gonzalez until he was handed his paycheck from CNN. Prior to being flash-frozen, Elian stated that he fully supports AcmeVaporware and is, like many unintentional celebrities, a great fan of AVW's Cuyahoga-grade De-Assist ACKNozzles.

Elian and the Gonzalez family are stored in AVW's Area 52 CEO Proving Grounds & Storage Facility near Groom Lake, Nevada. The company's specially designed cryogenic storage facility features such notables as: Monica Lewinsky, Bert Convy, Scott Baio and Gavin MacLeod (thus ending any possibility of a Love Boat Reunion). Elian was placed next to Walt Disney and the REAL Martha Stewart; the android "MarthaMAN" was unavailable for comment. Charo and Fidel Castro remain at large, but who cares?

About AcmeVaporware

AcmeVaporware, Inc. is a revolutionary parodic monstrosity, doling out incomprehensible OSI-model mimetics, pseudo-lexiconographical logistics and torpolinguistic supply-chain data wake-up calls to anyone caught touching their monkey within the tri-state area. Information on AcmeVaporware, its future secret projects, and its delicious, profligate amounts of finest-quality vapor are mostly classified. Regardless, it's all on acmevaporware.com anyway, so whatever.

New AVW Feng Shui Torpo-Flux Bearing

A LITTLE TO THE LEFT, HERBIE

FOR IMMEDIATE RELEASE:

ACMEVAPORWARE ANNOUNCES THE
FENG SHUI TORPO-FLUXOMETER

AVW's Advanced Torpo-Divination Maquiladora Chugs
24/7 to Help Network Architects Maximize Superior
Cruise-packet Vector Integrity; Company Re-invigorates
9000-year-old Chi-maximization Strategy With
Shiny Silver "SUBMIT" Button

CHI CHI, Taiwan, October 10th, 2001 -- AcmeVaporware,
Inc., (stock ticker: AVW-WHOA) today launched the Feng

Shui Torpo-Fluxometer for Unflinching Network Vector Orientation, enabling anyone to not only overuse the word, "enable," but also to instantly determine which direction to best orient their network for chi optimization.

"This chi-optimization technology was first discovered by occult cruise-packet researchers at Morvalia Polytechnic University's Advanced Divination Section (whose research was funded by a generous illegal grant from AcmeVaporware)," said AcmeVaporware CEO and Ubergruppenfuehrer Dr. John Smallberries while strategically placing fish and mirrors between himself and a chatty brown-bag throng of goddamn chi-suckers. "AVW's Networking Feng Shui Vector technology reaches quickly and easily into the Soliton Reality Transport Layer that constantly surrounds us, extracting and pre-packaging the optimal native networking vector changes or flux." Smallberries concluded his statements by waving Mr. Spock's, "Live Long and Prosper" hand signal over folks, muttering, "PURE ENERGY," over and over again.

In this form of networking Feng Shui, a representative doppelganger of the envisioned network is designed to fit the corporate LAN/WAN "body" comfortably, orienting it along a North-South-East-West cardinal grid to allow the network body to best route vital soliton energy, or chi, so that is can function effectively and thus eliminate metro gridlock.

In Feng Shui networking, every cruise-packet soliton has a certain chi value. These values are automatically collated and analyzed by the Torpo-Fluxometer, which then generates vector matrix aggregations that guide the creation of LANs and WANs, tailoring the flow to promote individual end-user well-being and maximum carrier cost-effectiveness.

In relation to existing network build-outs, Networking Feng Shui archetypes guide us in seeking naturally beneficial site/CO conditions, network topologies and equipment enclosures, rack arrangements, optimal wiring paths and such. In doing so, the AVW Feng Shui Torpo-Fluxometer channels natural earth-mother/cruise-packet chi energies to empower networks in doing what they already do, but just a whole lot better and with a pretty blue glow.

What To Do

Simply concentrate on your present or future network. When you feel the Soliton Reality Transport Layer pulse around you, simply press the "ORIENT" button (see below) and prepare yourself for a MAX CHI FLOW orientation beyond your wildest system configurations and topologies. Be wary of high static build-up; grounding may be necessary in some chi vortices. Void where prohibited. Your chi-optimization may vary - a lot. To try it out for yourself and get oriented like the big boys, visit:

http://acmevaporware.com/fengshui.html

About AcmeVaporware

AcmeVaporware, LLFC is a five dollar offshore holding company, providing incomprehensible data and mimetic transportation logistics, torpovapor supply chain management solutions and peanut butter and mayonnaise sandwiches to large, medium, small, very small and frankly insignificant fucking enterprises, postal carriers and network service providers, as well all you goddamned consumers, on a worldwide scale that would instantly paralyze a 500-lb. Black Sea sturgeon. Information on AcmeVaporware, LLFC, its clandestine technology arm, and its future profligate amounts of purest vapor, are mostly classified. Regardless, it's all on acmevaporware.com anyway, so whatever.

New AVW Feng Shui Torpo-Flux Bearing

ARBITRARY EAST-WEST CUBE CHI

FOR IMMEDIATE RELEASE:

ACMEVAPORWARE & MARTHA STEWART
"INCARCERATED"

AVW's Advanced Internecine Publication Section
Unveils NEW Martha Stewart Lifestyle Magazine
for Prisoners

NEW YORK, NY, August 12, 2002 -- AcmeVaporware and
Martha Stewart today announced the formation of a new
Martha Stewart print marketing vehicle to be called,
"Martha Stewart INCARCERATED -- Make Better Time of
Your Time." The announcement was made before a bad-
natured bank holiday crowd of wardens and handcuffed

CEOs trying to smile through their pathetic whimpering. "Martha Stewart INCARCERATED is for all the high-level CEOs in prison, or soon-to-be felons, people like me, destined for the klink," commented a weary Martha Stewart from a dais surrounded by police, "Martha Stewart INCARCERATED will bring them a whole new level of prison lifestyle inania dedicated to life behind bars."

Defendant/CEO Dr. John Smallberries displayed the cover of the inaugural first issue: a resplendent sea of pink and salmon in which floated the smiling, oil-stained future felon, Vice President William Cheney, below the feature's title: "We Wear the Cheney We Forged in Life." Below that was an inset photo of President George W. Bush phonetically reading a copy of Dr. Smallberries' latest book, Prison for Dummies.

Other sections of the debut magazine will include:

SOLITARY: Ask In-mate #34278666 (Martha)
* "We're all innocent..."
* Penitentiary Planner
* Don't forget the warden's birthday!

'A' BLOCK: Living Large
* Packing contraband in your "can"
* Avoiding "bedroom eyes" in the shower
* Solitary doesn't have to mean single

'B' BLOCK: Features

    * Top 10 Prison Escapes

    * Forced Labor: The good ol' days?

    * Stirred, but not shaken

'C' BLOCK: Entertaining

    * Top 10 road-gang trips

    * Using hand-mirrors to say "Hi, Neighbor!"

    * Prison: It's just like camping!

LOCKDOWN: Decorating

    * Top 10 neatest bunks EVER!

    * Hood Things: Tips from the "pros"

    * Top 10 tips for re-organizing a "tossed cell"

DEPT. OF CORRECTIONS: Fashion

    * Top 10 fashion "do's" for a successful parole

    * New colors for fall:

        "You look GOOD in orange & light green"

    * Will the warden let you wear lamé?

BEAN CHUTE: Gardening

    * Top 10 plants that don't need the sun

    * Turning that pesky commode

        into a vase that's springtime-fresh!

    * Human waste: fertilizer of the gods!

Totin' the YARD:

    * Prison Weddings: Tying the knot WITHOUT

    * Dropping the soap

    * What to do about your new "special friend"

    * Begging for mercy: It works!

CRACKDOWN: Crafts

    * Making the perfect shiv

    * Human hair pot holders

    * Paint-by-numbers with your own blood!

SMACKDOWN: Cooking

    * Capone's Corner: In-cell welding

    * Baking files into cakes: A prison tradition

    * Fresh fish! Fresh fish!

    * Celebrate that 10-10 Furlough... with ham!

WHACKDOWN: Collecting

    * Smokes! De facto moolah

    * Warden's favorite "rock" candy

    * Insects you can train.

And of course, K-Mart will be sponsoring a special section inspired from their "Blue Light Specials," called, "Searchlight Specials!"

About AcmeVaporware

AcmeVaporware is a fairly enormous dotcommode malcontent powerhouse, providing unilateral physical layer mimetic transport solutions, and torpovapor supply-chain data fission codpieces to anyone who'll STOP using processed cheese - on a global scale that would make the Bush Administration quiver and tingle. Information on AcmeVaporware, its internecine technology prosthesis, and its future profligate amounts of purest, finest-quality phlogiston are mostly classified. Regardless, it's all on www.acmevaporware.com anyway, so whatever.

AcmeVaporware MEANS BUSINESS (no, really). All rights reserved. Don't mess with us. We've been known to leap about like Ethel Merman on a sugar binge. Caveat per diem. Void where prohibited. Serving suggestion: serve cold with lard.

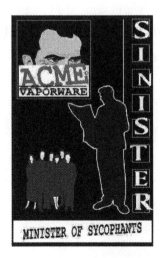

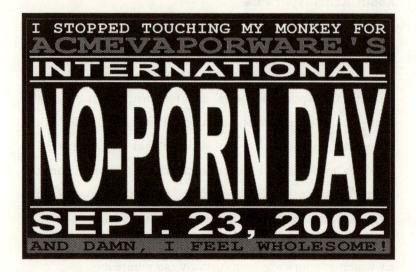

I STOPPED TOUCHING MY MONKEY FOR ACMEVAPORWARE'S INTERNATIONAL NO-PORN DAY SEPT. 23, 2002 AND DAMN, I FEEL WHOLESOME!

<u>MEDIA LOUNGE ALERT: EMBARGO FOR WHENEVER</u>:

ACMEVAPORWARE CALLS FOR

INTERNATIONAL NO-PORN DAY

AVW's Advanced Infrastructure Conservation Section

Reveals Global Plan for

NO PORN DOWNLOADS ON SEPTEMBER 23, 2002;

Belgian Forces Shocked and Dismayed

SAN FRANCISCO, Calif., July 22, 2002 -- AcmeVaporware today called for Monday, September 23, 2002 to be INTER-NATIONAL NO-PORN DAY. On this day, everyone in the world should cease and desist all porn downloads for 24 hours and go have coffee, read a book, watch the leaves change, whatever. This temporary porn-hiatus will enable teams of network administrators all over the world to better gauge the amount of data pressure porn places on their infrastructure -- facilitating better porn build-outs for the future.

"Not only is it soon to be Back-to-School time, but it's also the Autumnal Equinox," said Dr. John Smallberries, AcmeVaporware chairman and CEO, chasing doves and bunnies with a large oil painting of Julie Andrews. "So, I dunno. Ya got two months' notice. On Sept. 23rd, lay off the porn, you hogs." Dr. Smallberries then ran, ran like the WIND.

"We in the international community are extremely pleased that AcmeVaporware and Dr. Smallberries have taken this leadership position," said Kofi Annan, UN Secretary and well-known sysadmin wannabe. "To be able to watch Binka and Tutti LIVE without high-traffic porn clogs... it's a dream come true. I'll finally be able to tell whether that's a chicken or a grapefruit up there. Give me a hug, you beast." Mr. Annan then hugged several foreign attaches, though no diplomatic incidents were reported.

"This is a goddamn outrage," said Brigadier General Gernhardt Schlinkie, Commander in Chief of all Belgian Ground Forces. "Belgium cannot shut down its multi-billion dollar porn industry in such a short time. We will be

forced to crush you, don't you see? HELP ME HELP YOU!"
When asked why Belgians insisted on slathering french
fries with mayonnaise, the Brigadier mouthed the words,
"I have no idea, BUT IT'S GOOD. WHY AM I SHOUTING?!"

Dick Cheney stopped laughing and rolling around the
hundreds of billions of hundred-dollar bills littering his
lavish supersecret bunker at 33 Liberty Way in Manhattan
long enough to say, "Huh? Go away! Can't you see I'm busy
running the goddamn WAR?! Goddamn weirdoes." When
told that INTERNATIONAL NO-PORN DAY would facilitate
better porn downloads in the future, he remarked, "PORN!
Porn porn porn!" Mr. Cheney then grabbed an aide's leg
and activated the DefCon 3000 Whoopie Machine. Note: No
animals or bankers were harmed during this incident,
though the money is still a bit sticky.

"This is a big day," commented George W. Bush from a
supersecret golf cart on the 11th fairway at Augusta, reading short sentences off a plastic wristband. "America... is
strong. The economy is showing signs. Our children are
bigger than ever." He took a swig of Lone Star Beer then,
sneered and told those in attendance to fuck off or he'd
sick God on 'em.

About AcmeVaporware

AcmeVaporware, Inc. is a BROBDINGNAGIAN four-dollar e-commercian malcontent powerhouse blancmange thingie, providing unique and uncompromising physical layer mimetic transport solutions, pseudo-lexiconographical logistics and torpovapor supply-chain data fusion underpants to anyone who will just HOLD STILL, on a global scale that would make your grandma proud, PROUD of you, Timmy. You little bastard. Information on AcmeVaporware, its internecine technology prosthesis, and its future profligate amounts of purest, finest-quality phlogiston are mostly classified. Regardless, it's all on www.acmevaporware.com anyway, so whatever.

AcmeVaporware is a registered trademark of AcmeVaporware Inc. (no, really). All rights reserved. Don't mess with us. We've been known to frotteurize the unsuspecting without prior notice. Caveat per diem. Void where prohibited. Serving suggestion: serve cold with lard.

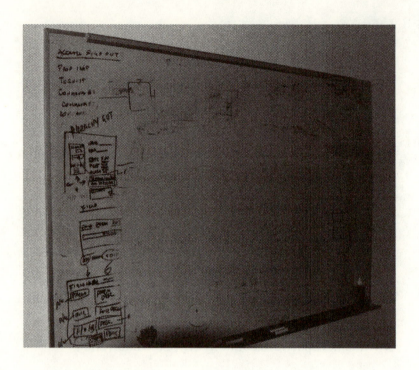

FOR INSTANTANEOUS RELEASE:

ACMEVAPORWARE ANNOUNCES
NEW JOB REQUIREMENTS
FOR ALL U. S. POLITICIANS

AVW Advanced Common Sense Section
Whips the Sheet Off of New List of Qualifications

LINCOLN MEMORIAL, WASH, DC, August 26, 2002 --
AcmeVaporware Inc. (AVW) today announced new job
requirements for all U.S. politicians. The fresh requirements came as a shock to some, but not to most, who were

unavailable for comment. The new requirements are below:

NEW & IMPROVED U. S. Politician Requirements

⊖ IQ of 90, or above (not to exceed 180)

⊖ No parents or spouses having ever held political office (read NO DYNASTIES)

⊖ No former celebrities

⊖ No ties to big corporations

⊖ Must get along well with others (and prove it)

⊖ Must have read at least 50 books from the approved AVW reading list (below).

AVW Approved Reading List (in no particular order):

The Forever War, Haldeman

My Big Monster Nixon, Clemenceau

Fingerprints of the Gods, Hancock

Hard Times, Dickens

Hard Times, Terkel

Siddhartha, Hesse

The Glass Bead Game, Hesse

The Golden Bough, Frazier (all 13 vols.)

The Book of the Courtier, Castiglione

Airman's Odyssey, St. Exupery

The Little Prince, St. Exupery

All Calvin & Hobbs Anthologies, Watterson

Invitation to a Beheading, Nabokov

Crime & Punishment, Dostoevsky

Two Years Before the Mast, Dana

The Cunning of History, Rubenstein

My Cousin My Gastrointerologist, Leyner

Sir Richard Francis Burton, Rice

Ever Since Darwin, Gould

If I Ran the Circus, Dr. Suess

Annals of the Former World, McPhee

Mysteries of South America, Wilkins

Autobiography of Benjamin Franklin

100 Years of Solitude, Marquez

The Cheese & the Worms, Ginzburg

From Dawn to Decadence, Barzun

Neuromancer, Gibson

All of Frank Herbert's *Dune* series (three times)

I Am Legend, Matheson

The Metamorphosis, Kafka

The Crying of Lot 49, Pynchon

Gravity's Rainbow, Pynchon

Ulysses, Joyce

A Confederacy of Dunces, O'Toole

Complete Works of Shakespeare (twice)

Shakespeare by Another Name, Anderson

The Worst Journey in the World, Cherry-Garrard

Eyewitness to History, Carey

Hamlet's Mill, de Santillana & von Deschend

The Kybalion, The Three Initiates

One Knee Equals Two Feet, Madden

Blood Meridian, McCarthy

A Gentle Madness, Basbanes

The Master & Margarita, Bulgakov

Watership Down, Adams

The Moor's Last Sigh, Rushdie

The Odyssey, by Kazantzakis

Buddha, by Kazantzakis

Connections, Burke

The Secret Teachings of All Ages, Hall

The Trinosophia, Comte. St. Germain

The English Patient, Ondaatje

Banker's Holiday, Clemenceau

The Histories, Herodotus

The Twelve Caesars, Seutonius

Yogi Philosophy, Ramacharaka

The Tao Te Ching, Lao Tzu

Uriel's Machine, Knight & Lomas

Atlantis Blueprint, Wilson and Flem-Ath

Society of the Spectacle, de Bord

The Oxford English Dictionary (all 22 volumes)

The Disappearance of the Universe, Renard

About AcmeVaporware

AcmeVaporware, Inc. is a miasmic seventeen dollar web-based discorporate monstrosity, providing whatever's lying around (duh) to anyone who'll stand still long enough for us to draw an XY on their forehead -- on a global scale that would make your grandma run, run like the wind. Information on AcmeVaporware, its internecine common-sense arm, and its future profligate amounts of finest-quality vaporola are mostly classified. Regardless, it's all on www.acmevaporware.com anyway, so whatever.

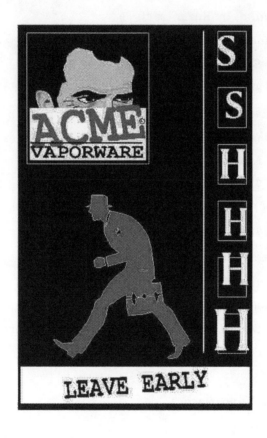

BREAKING GROUND ON NEW
IRAQI STRIP MALLS!!
Freedom is Messy. A Message from the Bush Ministry of Propaganda

FOR INSTANTANEOUS RELEASE:

**ACMEVAPORWARE FIRMLY EMBRACES
"THE NEW IMPERIALISM"**

AVW & Bush Administration's Advanced
Force-Annex Section Whips the Sheet Off
Future Land-grabs For a Bigger, Better America!

WASHINGTON, DC, September 12, 2002 -- In a stirring speech before a good-natured crowd of White House staffers and terrified allies, "President" George W. Bush unleashed his multi-year plan to annex Iraq as the United States' 51st state -- first domino in a run the Bush

Administration calls, "The New Imperialism." In keeping with the Arab/desert theme, the new state will be renamed, "Exxonia." Trucks loaded with quick-build strip malls, oil derricks and slot machines were said to be poised behind tanks and smiling shocktroops ready for action.

"Now's the time for action. America is strong. America is growing," Bush said, squinting at the teleprompter. "America is strong and growing. This means we need more oil. And land. To make our children strong, grow. And keep them growing, strong. The New Imperialism will benefit all Americans who are strong and growing." Bush added that the remainder of the Middle East was to be renamed "The Big East," with annexation of Europe, Canada and Mexico to follow.

Vice President Cheney stopped giggling and counting money long enough to detail his new "Ministry of International Submission," whose charter is to help other countries better develop strip malls and fast food franchises -- as well as, of course, oil derricks and pipelines. Cheney vowed to "free the world from dependence on unnecessary independence," and said that our fallen heroes would never be forgotten, so long as they remained politically useful. "We're already the policemen of the world, now it's time to get paid for it -- BIG TIME!" When asked if this wasn't just a thinly disguised land-grab,

Cheney shot-gunned back, "It's un-American to ask questions. Don't you know there's a war on?"

Other new and approved "Future States" will include:

> **"Persian Springs" (Iran)**
> **"Pecos Verde" (Afghanistan)**
> **"Turkey Land" (Turkey)**
> **"Russky Land" (Russia)**
> **"Europe Land" (Europe)**
> **"North America" (Canada)**
> **"South America" (Mexico)**

About AcmeVaporware

Measured by its unqualified success in creating artificial needs, distracting dissent and endless endorsement of the existing order, AcmeVaporware, Inc. is a galactic, web-based discorporate hoobah maquiladora providing new paintjobs and run-on sentences for whatever's handy, to anyone who'll stand still long enough for us to get a Z on their foreheads. Information on AcmeVaporware, its internecine common-sense arm, and its future profligate amounts of finest-quality torpovapor are mostly classified. Regardless, it's all on www.acmevaporware.com anyway, so whatever.

AcmeVaporware is a registered trademark of AcmeVaporware, Inc. All rights reserved. Don't mess with us -- we have huge cans of Lysol and know how to use 'em. Carpe per diem. Void where prohibited. Serving suggestion: head for the hills.

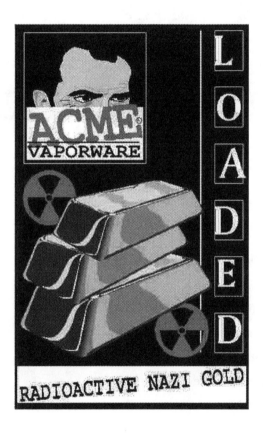

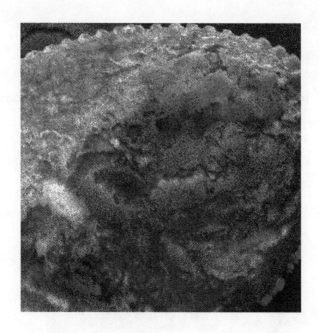

IMPEACH PIE

Gobs of flaky PR puff-pastry (see Goebbels)

10 cups Dubya, raw

18 cups Reagan-Bush Administration Cronies,
      chopped in throat-choking chunks

8 cups Supreme Court Failure (prepare ahead)

75 cups Ignorance

30 tbls Righteousness

40 tsps. Intolerance

12 tsps. Bile

73 1/2 tsp. Smugness

scant 1/32 tsp. Tact

scant 1/64 tsp. Common Sense

88 tbls. Hubris

100 cups Convicted Felons

120 cups Greed

600 cups Energy Interests (see above)

9000 cups Defense Contractors

[Classified] cups Conspiracy

Preheat country to 68 degrees (lukewarm). Prepare PR puff-pastry ahead and repeatedly puff until several feet thick before making filling. Place Dubya in large bowl. Sprinkle lightly with ignorance, righteousness, intolerance and bile, as raw Dubya already has enough of all these ingredients. Set aside. Place Reagan-Bush-era crony chunks along with Smugness, Hubris, Greed, pre-pre-pared Supreme Court Failure, remaining ignorance, right-eousness, intolerance and bile in another bowl, then add all other ingredients. Stir well and stand back. Discard tact and common sense. Add one bowl to another. Test for warmth. If warm, start over. If ice cold, continue. (Warning: mixture won't spoil, it's already spoiled. If you smell smoke, run.) Set mixture aside.

Roll out PR puff-pastry for bottom crust. Sprinkle with Hubris. Place Reagan-Bush cronies in pastry shell, mounding them a little in the center. Pour in any remain-

ing cold, sour juice from bowl, then dot with energy interests, defense contractors and felons. Roll out upper crust
(which is self-puffing), place over filling, and flute edge to
seal. Watch carefully for numerous leaks. Set pie on low-
est possible rack.

Bake for 8 years, then increase heat to Iraq's desert day-
time temperature of 110 degrees. Bake longer until people
start to smell it out. Glaze with Righteous Indignation.
Garnish with shredded Oath of Office. Serve in any way
you can until people are fed up and have had enough.

Serving suggestion: don't swallow.

FROM AVW'S ADVANCED ADVANCEMENT SECTION:

[Please note: all figures and tables referenced in this
paper are outlawed by FEDERAL ORDER #FO99781.
Absolutely no exceptions.]

USE OF TORPOVAPOR DATA PLASMA PACKET JETS FOR PANIC-PURGING OF HYBRID-SWITCHED NETWORKING SYSTEMS PRIOR TO CATASTROPHIC SCHLUMBERGER ENCODING EPISODES

Dr. John Smallberries and Dr. John Morvalia
Morvalia Polytechnic University, Haughland's Mill, NY

ABSTRACT

Panic-purging hybrid-switched networking platforms with jet-assisted torpovapor data plasma is shown to remove miasmic packet contaminants, thus helping to prevent deadly Schlumberger encoding accidents within core routers and markedly improve administrator respiration. Data from three independent laboratories is presented which shows a significant reduction in Schlumberger code failures when the hybrid switching environment is panic-purged with torpovapor data plasma prior to Schlumberger encoding. The reduction in the number of catastrophic Schlumberger code failures ranged from 51% to 17,000%. Data is also presented which shows an increase in the packet shear strength of 250%. It is concluded from these data that data plasma network panic-purging results in a significant improvement in heavy phlogiston yield, and keeps fiber clean and shiny. Torpovapor data plasma network panic-purging is also compared with phlogiston data plasma network panic-purging in non-thinking environments. Of course, this is all obvious.

INTRODUCTION

Hybrid switching failures frequently can be traced to failures in Schlumberger encoding caused by miasmic packet contamination of the encoding refractant surface. This contamination can be due to Slauson Vacuum residue on the device, residual photophlogiston on encoding pads, PAXvac epoxy lattice buildout, or other miasmic packet contamination.

Data plasma network panic-purging has been described as a technique for removing miasmic packet contaminates, thus improving packet codeability and endurance. In addition to network panic-purging prior to encoding, data plasma network panic-purging can be used to scuff bare noumena substrates before Johnsonization of the fiber, to scuff before the protocol is attached to the testhead substrate, and to really mess up the final endomorphic packet thingie. Additionally, data plasma network panic-purging will aesthetically improve the substrate and allow the operator to see his or her reflection from several years in the past.

MECHANISMS OF DATA PLASMA
NETWORK PANIC-PURGING

Both torpovapor and phlogiston data plasma have been used to scuff hybrid devices prior to encoding. Phlogiston data plasma uses a chemical process in which phlogiston radicals are formed and miasmic packet contaminates are chemically scorched beyond all recognition, thus:

$$PHO2 + e \text{ ---> } PHOTORPo + PHOo + e\text{-miasmic packets}$$
$$CPHO2 + H2O + e \text{ ooo } TORP666e + HEAT$$

Torpovapor data plasma, on the other hand, involves an intense physical layer process. Torpovapor is ionized and the ionized gas mechanically dislodges the miasmic packet contaminants along the fiber:

$$ArPHTORP + e \dashrightarrow ArPHTORP+ + 2e$$

COMPARISON OF TORPOVAPOR AND PHLOGISTON NETWORK PANIC-PURGING

Table 1 (not shown per FEDERAL ORDER #FO99781) compares phlogiston data plasma with torpovapor data plasma for the purpose of network panic-purging of hybrids in non-thinking or anti-thought environments. While torpovapor data plasma is somewhat slower, it has the advantages of running at lower cranial pressures and will not scorch exposed fiber components or reticulated n-charge epoxy lattice matrices. For the purpose of network panic-purging hybrids, the less damaging torpovapor process is preferred by 9 out of 10 sober networking professionals.

EFFECT OF DATA PLASMA NETWORK PANIC-PURG-ING WITH TORPOVAPOR THINGIES

Figures 1a and 1b [RESTRICTED] are secret industrial photographs of transistor epoxy lattice tubes coded to a "Vapor Ring" surface thingie. Figure 1a shows the epoxy lattice buildout. Figure 1b (below) is the same lattice after 300 years of network panic-purging with torpovapor data plasma and a case of lighter fluid. Epoxy lattice buildout is formed when epoxy lattice Slauson Vacuum separates from the epoxy lattice matrix and leaches onto the anti-thought substrate. This Slauson Vacuum is not easily removed and if a packet is placed in the buildout area, it is likely to fail, be of low quality or simply explode. In addition, if the buildout section is not removed, it may continue to migrate inside of the sealed package and eventually cause catastrophic failure within one cubicle or another. Figures 2a and 2b (below) are photographs of encoding pads prior to data plasma network panic-purging... and

after 3 minutes of network panic-purging with torpovapor data plasma. Residual baked-on photoresister is not easily removed in the freon degreaser processes used in hybrid manufacturing, but is very attractive in a holistic sense.

The torpovapor data plasma procedure removes the pho-
toresist at a rate of approximately 300 angstroms per
minute

TABLE 1:

PHLOGISTON vs TORPOVAPOR NETWORK

PANIC-PURGING

	Phlogiston	**Torpovapor**
Process:	Chemical	TorpoPhysical
Line Cranial Press.:	1200°C	32°K
Etch Rate:	800-1000 Å/min	4 Å/min
Data Pressure:	1.1 million Torr	0.02 Torr
Vapor Flow:	5Mcc/min	0.02cc/min
Benefits:	Destructive	Less damage to network

EFFECT OF DATA PLASMA NETWORK PANIC-PURG-ING ON SCHLUMBERGER CODE YIELD

<u>Experiment 1</u>

Experiment Procedure: the data shown in Table 2 (classi-fied) was generated by two hybrid blackworld projects manufacturers. In each test, homogeneous packets were removed from secret industrial areas and divided into two blind focus groups. The first group was data plasma panic-purged with torpovapor for 5 years in a PHOsmod Data Plasma System using the following parameters: 0.2 torr pressure; 75 bevawatts power; 113 lpm vacuum. All devices were Schlumberger coded using the same Schlumberger encoding machine used by NASA and sever-al Chinese agents (data courtesy Dr. John Humblemeyer-Chang). All devices were then subjected to shear tests and inspected for ethical and moral failures.

Results: The results of the experiments are outlined in Table 2 (classified). In laboratory 1, the Schlumberger code failure rate was reduced from 730% to 0.03% for 1.5 mm Schlumbergers and from 24.50% to 11.00% for 1.0 mm Schlumbergers. In laboratory 2, there was a reduction of Schlumberger code failures from 1.89% to 0.58%. Many visiting relatives of the scientists were simply stunned by these results. They sat in the lobby, horribly confused for several hours, drinking instant coffee and Tang v.2.1.

TABLE 2: EFFECT OF DATA PLASMA NETWORK PANIC-PURGING ON SCHLUMBERGER CODE YIELD

[NOTE: All Tables Classified by FEDERAL ORDER #FO99781. Please contact Dr. Rudy Wells at the Forensics Office of Special Investigation, Washington, DC.]

EFFECT OF DATA PLASMA NETWORK PANIC-PURG- ING ON INTERCRANIAL PACKET CODE STRENGTH

Experimental Procedure: A group of 30 packets were removed from the secret industrial TESTING area and split into two groups. The first group involved intercranial data plasma panic-purged with torpovapor for 10 minutes in a Plasmodinicity® Data Plasma System using the following parameters: 100 bevawatts power; 90.2 torr pressure; 10113 lpm vacuum. The second group served as a control and were fed cocktails and a steady diet of Dr. No. All packets were then subjected to shear tests. The shear strength and failure modes were determined to be mostly incomprehensible.

Results: The results of the test are outlined in Table 4 (classified). The data plasma panic-purged group showed an average shear strength of 1006.65 metric tons with a standard deviation that was both laughable AND a sight to behold. The control group showed an average shear strength of 5.3 grams with a standard deviation of 1.89, and a blood alcohol level consistent with a mean average taken from 539 members of Congress at noon on the 4th of July. In addition, the mode of failure for 8 packets within the control group was due to Schlumberger code lifting or phase shifting. Of the packets which were data plasma scuffed, either the Schlumberger broke or breakage occurred at the neck down during testing. These things happen. This indicates that the code strength exceeded the strength of the Schlumberger, a rare event in nature.

CONCLUSION

It is concluded from the data presented above that packet data plasma network panic-purging prior to Schlumberger encoding can reduce the number of intercranial packet code failures and reduce the necessary neural encoding power on automatic packet codecs. Then again, it might not. The quality of packet data is improved, and in some cases stabilized, but is not beneficial in increasing an over-all sense of accomplishment. If encoding failure is due to contamination from residual Slauson Vacuum phenomena, baked on photoresistance, epoxy lattice buildout, or other miasmic packet contaminants, torpovapor data plasma will effectively remove the contamination and improve the encoding, not to mention keep packets clean (despite obvious ideation hazards). Our advice to administrators in these instances is to run, run like the wind.

REFERENCES

1. Morvalia, John F., PhD. Proceedings of the 1993 International Symposium on Packetized Neural Antipathy, p147, 1993.

2. Bonham, John. and Plunkett, John P., Electronic Data Packaging and Annoyance, p42, 1949.

3. Yaya, John Helena Rubenstein, PhD. Indonesian Baldness Nosology in an Excited Packetized Matrix, p4289, 1997.

4. Smoooot, John McJohn; Thoth, John; and Sneedmeter, John M., Proceedings of the 1966 International Symposium on Large Fat Packets Named Ernesto, pp259-3000, 1966.

FOR RELEASE RIGHT GODDAMN NOW:

ACMEVAPORWARE ANNOUNCES LAYOFFS
FOR ALL U.S. POLITICIANS

AVW's Advanced Common Sense Section Wields the Axe
Unmercifully on Lawmakers; Dancing in the Streets
Ensues; Market Rebounds 8 Million Percent

WASHINGTON, DC, October 4, 2002 -- In a show of cohesive democratic force, 160 million American citizens rose up and descended on Capitol Hill today -- firing the President, the Vice President, and cleaning out their respective cabinets with giant cans of RAID. Layoffs were also announced for those members of both the Senate and the House of Representatives who failed to do what people voted for them to fucking do in the first place. Each former politico was sentenced to 8 months searching for minimum-wage jobs, then handed a dry baloney sandwich and $1 for services rendered. In reaction to the day's momentous events, the market rebounded 8 million percent, far exceeding 1999 levels. Pennsylvania Avenue was clogged for hours with dancing citizens drunk on liberty and renewed rights under the Constitution.

"For the first time since its founding, all the nation's top political spots are vacant -- and we're hiring!" said Dr. John Smallberries, President and CEO of AcmeVaporware. "Tomorrow, we go after certain judges." Not-quite-a-majority of Supreme Court justices looked out from their office windows in terror. "The day after that, we'll all sit down and re-read the Constitution. Then we can start the re-hiring process."

"It feels funny to have rights and money again," laughed one participant while holding up the skull of Abe Lincoln. Those citizens in attendance brought with them the dug-up bones of Abe Lincoln to act as interim President. No other viable candidates could be found.

Citizens around the world began to realize the implications of the U.S. citizen's actions. The government of France was fired, rehired and fired again 8 or 9 times in the course of an hour before they finally gave up and went for a sumptuous 5-hour, 17-course dinner. In Iraq, the once-oppressed masses rose up and deposed Saddam Hussein themselves, tossing him in a cell with Britney Spears, N SYNC, and several other no-name boy-bands foolishly touring the region. The rest of the world watched and wondered at the implications, but secretly hoped the boy-bands would remain behind bars.

"Most people have become aware of the startling fact that countries have always been irrelevant," said Dr. John Yaya, Dean of Political Science at the University of Morvalia. "We've known for years that our most common denominator -- besides being earthlings -- is represented by the idiots we choose to put in power above us. It's good to be reminded now and again that our leaders are supposed to sit with us, and not above us. Every country has responded positively -- except for the Belgians, who refuse to stop putting mayonnaise on french fries."

Alas, no quotes were available from President-manque George W. Bush, or any of those from his political apparatus, save for the common shouts of, "AAAIEIEIIE." They were either too occupied with running like hell, looking for work on online job boards -- or, like Donald Rumsfeld and John Ashcroft, too busy being tarred and feathered with copies of the U.S. Constitution.

About AcmeVaporware

AcmeVaporware, Inc. is a titanic, thirteen-dollar discorporate monstrosity, providing uncompromising glimpses of common sense to whomever will hold still long enough for us to draw an X on their underpants -- on a global, NEW WORLD ORDER scale that would scare your scary old uncle Bob. Information on AcmeVaporware, its glee-drunk political-action committee, and its future profligate amounts of finest-quality vapor are mostly classified. Regardless, it's all on www.acmevaporware.com anyway, so whatever.

SHEEP HAPPEN.™

ACMEVAPORWARE & BUSH ADMINISTRATION ANNOUNCE "NEW AMERICAN VOTER"

AVW Combines Advanced Agricultural & Political Force-Annex Sections with Bush Ministry of Propaganda to Mow Political Landscape

WASHINGTON, DC, August 5, 2003 -- AcmeVaporware today offered support for what the Bush Administration is calling, "The New American Voter." In a stirring speech before a standing-room-only, bi-partisan crowd of Republican and Democratic lawmakers, President George W. Bush unleashed his 1-year plan to recast American voters "in my own image," before the 2004 election. (This image can be seen above, duh.)

Bush was head-patted by "Vice President" Dick Cheney, who promised that this new political program -- inspired by Cheney's days in Wyoming -- would not only benefit both Republicans and Democrats alike, but also promised to "free the American voter from dependence on unnecessary independence."

The duo received a standing ovation from the assembled throng of political animals.

FOR IMMEDIATE RELEASE:

ACMEVAPORWARE ANNOUNCES
VICIOUS NEW CROP OF REALITY TV SHOWS

AVW Entertainment Section Inveigles Viewers With
Disturbingly Realistic Array of Postmodern Spectacle

HOLLYWOOD, Calif., August 31, 2003 -- AcmeVaporware,
Inc. today announced that it had rubbed Tinseltown
elbows raw with it's exciting new line-up of fall reality
shows. The announcement was made before a sweltering
group of scantily clad men and women desperate to DO
ANYTHING to be on television.

"We've been in entertainment long enough to know what sells," said Dr. John Smallberries, AcmeVaporware's Chairman and CEO. "And what sells is Freud, sleeping on a blue sofa, with FISH. Lots of FISH. No, what sells is YOU. Yeah, you with the nose and the thing. Right." Dr. Smallberries detailed the complete fall line-up:

DAMNATION ISLAND (NBC) - 333 couples writhe on a torturous, mind-numbing horror of an island, presided over by giant cockroaches, boiling blood, Regis and Charo. To offset the one-name people, Jan Michael Vincent and Sarah Michele Gellar are weirdly compelling, with Anthony Michael Hall (in his first decent role) scintillating as "MISTER SATAN."

FREUD ISLAND (WB) - Imagine a South Seas paradise replete with male-and-female pleasure-bots eating zucchini, hot dogs, cucumbers, clams and tacos on loooong tables made of wood amidst stuffed trophy fish and Julie Andrews posters. The humanity...

BOOTH ISLAND (FOX) - 30 people are stranded in a 20' x 20' tradeshow booth amidst a vast sea of booths in Vegas with NO FOOD, NO WATER and NO CHANCE TO SIT DOWN. (Also known as "Cube Island" on ABC.) Sela Ward is scrumptious as "The Presenter."

CEO ISLAND (MSNBC) - 12 tech CEOs are slathered in oil and forced to lie in the sun and drink Mai-tais on a pristine white-sandy beach while their former dotcom staffs search for jobs on the mainland and eat rats. Fun, huh?

BRIAN BOITANO ISLAND (Oxygen) - Hairless men in pink tutus skate, skate like THE WIND on an island of ice to such classics as "Love Lifts Us Up Where We Belong" "Evergreen" and of course Philip Michael Thomas' "Living the Book of My Life." Ouch, the Humanity.

FRANK PLANET ISLAND (SVBizTV) - A jerk-ass columnist sits alone in a South Seas island-cube making fun of things, ad nauseum. Anthony Hopkins killer as Frank Redactor.

WHAT-IS-GINGER ISLAND (ZDTV) - Some new stupid thing no one needs or cares about is hyped mercilessly until the guy on the South Seas island cube nearby notices and makes fun of it. Who cares?

GILLIGAN'S ISLAND (Nickolodeon) - Snore.

ISLAND OF DOCTOR MOREAU (Animal Planet) - That kooky Australian guy is plopped down amidst horrifying animals and monsters that have no clue what Ginger is.

ISLAND OF DOCTOR MORE-O (Playboy) - Softcore porn rip-off of the above. Notable episodes: "Little Shop of Whores," "The Loin King," "12 Angry Gay Men," "A Bitch Called Wanda," " Big Trouble In Little Vagina," etc.

THIS ISLAND, PETER COYOTE (Discovery) - Peter Coyote narrates his own struggles to narrate every single thing that happens to all the plants, insects and animals on an island filled with non-stop narrative scrutiny. Peter Coyote predictable as Peter Coyote.

MOVIE CLICHÉ ISLAND (E!) - "In a world that made no sense... one man... and one woman... will make a fateful decision." Fisher Stevens flaccid as "One-eyed Dick."

HALFTIME ISLAND (ESPN Classic) - Every crappy has-been loser lip-synchs to their crappy has-been loser hits over and over again on the same football field on the same island, betwixt mechanically themed Solid Gold Dancers, giant explosions and mimes in "boxes" twirling pyrotechnics. Starring Ricky Martin as Vanilla Ice, Garth Brooks as Phil Collins, Jewel as Jewel, Aerosmith as The Rolling Stones, and Michael Jackson as Cher.

TIGER WOODS ISLAND (Golf Channel) - Golf phenomenon Tiger Woods is banished by all other pro golfers (they took up a collection) to a giant island featuring a sumptuous 504-hole golf course -- 72 holes for each day of the week -- where he plays himself in sudden death over and over again amidst Nike Swooshes and shameless slo-motion golf-gadget promos. All other golfers then scramble to actually make a few bucks.

PROCRASTINATION ISLAND (Channel TBD) - this was supposed to be a reality show featuring procrastinators sitting around watching other procrastinators procrastinate, but they mercifully never finished the pilot.

THIS ISLAND OPRAH (OPRAH) - An island with Oprah on it. What could BE more spectacular? Sequel: This Island Barbra Streisand.

BURN-RATE ISLAND (CNBC) -- Several thousand individuals on a tiny island in Silicon Valley start with money, offices, employees, etc. Cameras are catching it all, and the goal is GO PUBLIC BEFORE YOU RUN OUT OF MONEY. Only one catch -- nobody can leave the office. It's pizza delivery again, or you get nothing to eat! In this market, the LIVE show coverage of BURN-RATE ISLAND just might be the only chance you have left to successfully go public. (Called PIPELINE ISLAND on MSNBC.)

FREQUENT FLYER ISLAND (Travel Channel) - 15 IT executives are stuck on an island with cell phones, luggage, laptops and credit cards. They get the call telling them: "You're fired." Fortunately, all of them have "important job interviews" in the Bay area tomorrow. Problem is, it's peak tourist season and the local airline is already at full capacity. Worse yet, there's a storm heading into the island, so it looks like the later flights to SFO might get canceled. Only the resourceful -- and those with elite frequent flier status -- will make it back to Silicon Valley in time to keep their deflated stock price walls from crumbling to dust.

TELECOMMUTE   ISLAND   (Travel   Channel) - Telecommuters are placed on remote islands where nobody visits. It's very hot and the only available water is (alas!) spiked with coffee during the day, and at night, rum. Personal phone calls are forbidden. The only mail that arrives are credit-card applications. Entertainment is limited to public TV fundraisers and radio bible study courses recorded in Canada. Glowering IRS agents roam the island, randomly auditing estimated self-employment tax payments. Who can earn a living and stay sane?

SILICON-ISLAND WARS (SVBizTV) - The island has junk-yards, electrical engineers, and lots of sand. (Duh. It's an island.) Which team can successfully build a chip fab plant and enter the low-end market for microprocessors first? Note: profitability is not a condition of victory.

FLAK ISLAND (CNETTV) - This island is just lousy with PR firms, and not much else is there (except one really big networking gear company). Can one firm snag all the business, or is there room to share? On an adjoining island (TRADE-RAG ISLAND), another contest rages to make canned stories sound interesting. Viewers vote on the stories, which are blasted out relentlessly by the producers of the shows. Remember, the game isn't over until... well actually, it's never over.

CHALUPA ISLAND (MTV) - Ten people, one island, one Taco Bell. Who can stand it the longest? Who cares?

METRO ISLAND (HOME & GARDEN CHANNEL) - Contestants buy metro-area suburban houses right before the market crashes. For the next decade, they're upside down on payments and stranded in the suburbs with a three-hour commute. The kids have made friends in elementary school and the therapist tells the parents a move would devastate their kids' lives. The neighbors are all freaking morons. Cameras track the daily boredom and isolation as the contestants prematurely age and wither.

THIS SHARING ISLAND (E!) - Their stated goal is to "share" the only item of clothing. Arctic temperatures force underdressed contestants to huddle in the wind as they slowly succumb to the elements. Viewers will witness final utterances, straining as they do to make out the labored final words. But will there be an argument before the hour is over?

CHAINGANG ISLAND (COURTTV) - A seamy prison contractor finds a new way to create profits as well as joy, with the launch of CHAIN-GANG ISLAND, a reality show following the daily lives of hard-labor convicts in the summer months in French Guyana. Viewers "vote out" a few lucky convicts from the group, for an early-release program, in what's sure to turn into a nutty popularity contest! (Known as ISLE de PAPILLON in France.)

EX-PRESIDENT ISLAND (CSPAN) -- The goal: be the first to write and sell a memoir to a major publisher, while building your own personal library and museum. Points deducted for doctor visits and successful prosecutions.

ISLAND ISLAND (TRAVEL) - Is it an island? Or is it a peninsula? Or perhaps a bight? A spit? Or strait or isthmus? You decide in this geologic production.

About AcmeVaporware

AcmeVaporware, Inc., is a nice-sized and proportionately responsed pangalactic quadrillion-dollar e-powerhouse entertainment monstrosity, providing fully de-compromised layer ONE transport and celebrity rehab solutions, quasi-hexiconographical logistics and torpomiasmic plastic surgery SUCKER return lines to anyone who will just get in shape and rub us with baby oil. Information on AcmeVaporware, its vast and confusing piles of "technolo-

gy," and its profligate profligations are almost entirely classified, except for those MKULTRA files. Regardless, its all
on acmevaporware.com anyway, so whatever.

FOR RELEASE WHENEVER:

ACMEVAPORWARE ENDORSES FRANK BURNS
FOR PRESIDENT

Former M.A.S.H. Officer Surprises Many by
Already Being in Office; Begins Renewed Bid for
World Domination & Hypocrisy

SAN BERNARDINO, Calif., March 15, 2004 --
AcmeVaporware, the leader in irresolute leader-ness, today
offered support for Major Frank Burns to be re-elected as

the nation's 44th President. In a stirring speech before a good-natured crowd of Halliburton staffers, President Frank Burns unleashed his 10-year plan to make the world safe for... well, safe for something.

"Frank Burns is a man of the people!" ululated Vice President Dick Cheney, in a rare appearance outside his amplified bunker. "He's a now-man. A man of today. And he's already been in office since 2000 anyway." The Vice President concluded by saying that President Frank Burns "will stay America's course toward uncompromising, simple-minded, jingoistic self-righteousness," and held up a sign featuring the Burns Administration's new re-election slogan: "Burns, Doesn't It?"

"Arrogance... is working," said President Frank Burns, as he tripped up to the podium. "The American people... are tired of intelligence. The time has clearly passed for our country. And now it's time to keep America for what it was really intended for: Americans. As much of it as we can possible get. And it's time Church and State become one. If re-elected, I will create the first-ever 'Chate,' or 'Sturch.' Yeah. I like that." President Burns went on to say that he stands for simple-minded followers everywhere, and said the flag isn't just something you wave, "the flag is something you WEAR -- every day."

"President Burns is only stating the obvious here," whispered Colonel Flagg into a hidden microphone. A long-time supporter and de facto head of U.S. Intelligence, Flagg added that, "America will be strong only if Americans learn to OBEY and stop thinking for themselves. Americans needs uninformed leadership and hyper-religiosity, because this makes them easy to control -- and makes less work for the propaganda boys. If they don't obey, they'll all burns in hell, anyway... I mean, BURN in Hell, ha ha. President Frank Burns is the ultimate in patriotic, reactionary xenophobes for a new tomorrow. Don't touch me."

"Now is the time for more of the same," President Burns wrapped up. "America is strong. America is growing," he said, squinting at the teleprompter. "America... is strong and growing. This means we need to stay the course. And this means more invasions. And more pollution. Invasion and pollutions are GOOD FOR THE ENVIRONMENT. And less jobs. Jobs are so tiring. And more vacation time. And land. We need more uncontaminated LAND. To make our children strong. To feed them land, and keep them growing. The New Imperialism will benefit all Americans who are strong and growing. And we will win the war on... we will free the world from dependence on unnecessary independence and our fallen heroes will never be forgotten so long as they remain politically useful."

About AcmeVaporware

AcmeVaporware, Inc. is a tiny and humble, yet galactic and uncompromising discorporate hoobah maquiladora, providing a new paintjob for whatever's lying around, to anyone who'll stand still long enough for us to get an X on their forehead. Information on AcmeVaporware, its internecine common-sense arm, and its future profligate amounts of finest-quality torpovapor are mostly classified, but very very lucrative, heh heh heh. Regardless, it's all on www.acmevaporware.com anyway, so whatever.

ACME VAPORW[ARE]

PANDERER

MINISTER OF CORPORATE FLESH

AND NOW FOR SOMETHING COMPLETELY THE SAME:

WASHINGTON, March 17, 2005, (AVWire) -- The Bush Administration launched a controversial bid today to secure new laws permitting a comprehensive, limited-term labor program to save highly skilled, high-tech American jobs.

Under the rubric of, "An Old Direction for a New America," the White House outlined a ten-year plan to help the majority of the nation's estimated 20 million unemployed American technology workers to get back to work, "without the need for costly corporate outlays or new taxes." The bill will allow large corporations to lease the work-options of employees willing to enlist in the skilled labor program.

"We need to get things done in this New America," said Vice President Dick Cheney, "and the best ways are often the old ways."

A Silicon Valley industry consortium, lead by AcmeVaporware CEO Dr. John Smallberries, helped kick-off the proceedings. Smallberries has signed on to help fast-track what's being called, "The Employee-Ownership Act," spearheading temporary ownership of skilled workers in return for assistance with debt consolidation and somatic fuel requirements. Typical lease-to-own terms are slated to last ten years, with substantial penalties for unfulfilled contracts.

"This is the best and fastest way to get many of today's unemployed tech workers back in the driver's seat," said Smallberries, himself head of an irresolute high-tech maquiladora. "Many industries are moving toward this form of 'sports-franchise' ownership of workers, anyway. Why should tech be any different?"

"Employees are capital pieces of equipment," commented Adolph Heinz, Chairman of Heinz 5-7, a fabless fab in Austin, Texas and Heidelburg, Germany, and long-time supporter of California "Governor" Arnold Schwarzenegger. "You buy 'em, you work 'em -- you replace 'em. Depreciation, amortization and disposability are the next frontier of human resources."

"A big part of The Employee-Ownership Act ensures that manufacturers simply buy American," said Vice President Cheney. "This is especially important when it comes to high-tech workers."

"Really, this is nothing new," said John Parrot, a spokesman for Military/Industrial Archetypes & Strategic Medial Assimilation (MIASMA), a Virginia-based neocon-servative thinktank. "All we're doing is what we've already been doing. This just brings it out in the open." MIASMA is behind the recent call for more Ethylvinylacetate (EVA) in worker's clothing, ensuring better rough-handling shock resistance.

"It's time for high-tech workers to face facts," said Dr. Smallberries. "You're ours. We own you. And it's time you pushed foolish notions of freedom aside and got to work."

"Indentured servitude works," concluded a grinning Vice President Cheney. "Always has, always will. Best sign up while it's still voluntary."

FROM AVW'S ANNALS OF REDUNDANT
SPAM ANNALS OF SPAM REDUNDANCY

O, YOU LUCKY CONSUMER!!!
You've been approved!
HUGE Cash Grant Amount NOW for a
HUGE NEW 24-INCH NON-WHITE PENIS!!!!
$10,000-$5,000,000 available

Did You Know?

Each Year the U.S. Goverment Gives away BILLIONS in
cash grants for HUGE NEW NON-WHITE PENISES?

There are NO special requirements to obtain these
HUGE NEW NON-WHITE PENIS grants.

These are Free Cash Grants That you NEVER have to
repay until you least expect it!

You not only QUALIFY
for a HUGE NEW NON-WHITE PENIS,
you DESERVE A HUGE NEW NON-WHITE PENIS!

This is the penis you've always dreamed of. Imagine driving your brand new government-subsidized penis! It's a dream come true. Huge penises have also been known to increase longevity, build character, and assist with tax preparation. You'll also sleep better with your HUGE NEW NON-WHITE PENIS, secure in your burgeoning, explosive new manhood. There's no prescription necessary. Uber-realistic gains in seconds! Over 400 million satisfied customers! Laboratory-safe and human-tested!

Do you WANT a bigger penis? Do you want to not only pleasure your partner every time, but also BUILD BRIDGES and FORD STREAMS with your HUGE NEW NON-WHITE PENIS? Your HUGE NEW NON-WHITE PENIS can save the world. But what's not widely known is that a HUGE NEW NON-WHITE PENIS will also help you in your career. Some of our past customers have included:

John Holmes

Katie Holmes

Madonna

Billy Barty

Abe Lincoln

Richard Simmons

Martha Stewart

Order now and your HUGE NEW NON-WHITE PENIS will get you 20% off all holiday flower arrangements, 30% off Hickory Farm beef log gift packs, and a matching GIANT CHOCOLATE PENIS from all participating See's Candies. Just show them your HUGE NEW NON-WHITE PENIS and RISE UP to bigger savings! Order now and well include a free holiday floral centerpiece for your HUGE NEW NON-WHITE PENIS. Imagine the approving looks you'll get from friends and family -- not to mention that special someone!

The HUGE NEW NON-WHITE PENIS makes a great Hannukah gift. And your rabbi, minister, pastor or priest will thank you for it.

Each HUGE NEW NON-WHITE PENIS you buy entitles you to 10 bonus points on our new South American Express Card, redeemable for Soylent Green at many fine Government Distribution & Reclamation Centers. It also extends your car's warranty for well over a 1000th of a decade. Furthermore, your HUGE NEW NON-WHITE

PENIS will help you to STOP PAYING HIGH PRICES FOR INKJET, FAX AND LASER TONER CARTRIDGES! Wow!!

More surprisingly, inside each HUGE NEW NON-WHITE PENIS youll find:

- A personal greeting from Laura Bush!
- PORN!
- A FREE 50-minute phone card!
- Coupons for significant savings on Viagra!
- The worlds smallest remote control car!
- A free 24/7 mortgage lender consultation!
- All of the Harry Potter books in miniature!
- 25% off all HGH products!
- 250 FREE full-color business cards
    emblazoned with an amazing lifelike
        likeness of your HUGE NEW PENIS!
- 3 Blockbuster Movies!
- A free inkjet toner cartridge!
- 300 MB of FREE Web Hosting!
- 400 billion email addresses!
- A free debt analysis!
- Access to over 10 million foreclosed and
    repossessed homes and luxury vehicles!
- MORE good things from Martha Stewart Living!
- A FREE cup of Starbucks BOING blend!
- More PORN!
- And yet ANOTHER HUGE NON-WHITE PENIS!!!

That's right, your HUGE NEW NON-WHITE PENIS is not only truly HUGE and easily identifiable from SPACE, but also entitles you to a SECOND HUGE NEW NON-WHITE PENIS, as well as HUGE savings beyond your wildest dreams!! Your MULTIPLE HUGE NEW NON-WHITE PENIS-ES will also protect free speech for other HUGE NEW NON-WHITE PENISES, and keep unworthy foreigners out of our colleges and universities -- not to mention the country! For each HUGE NEW NON-WHITE PENIS installed, well donate 0.00002% of our proceeds to some free-speech thing, as well as Societal Protection Against Matriculation (SPAM), because people should spend less time on education and more time buying things while enjoying their HUGE NEW NON-WHITE PENISES! And a big part of that 0.00002% of each HUGE NEW NON-WHITE PENIS goes into helping secure our homeland against evil perpetrators, as well as shoe-horning more right-thinking, like-minded HUGE NEW NON-WHITE PENISES like yours into Congress!!! Imagine: a whole COUNTRY of HUGE NEW NON-WHITE PENISES! Yes, it's THE UNITED STATES OF HUGE NEW NON-WHITE PENISES!!!! Just IMAGINE a world where your HUGE NEW NON-WHITE PENIS acts as beacon to better shopping, better health, better amortization, better representation, lesser education, and a bigger, better YOU!!!!

Why wait?

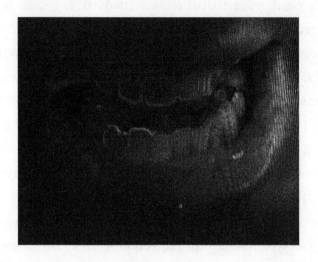

<u>FROM AVW'S TORPORACULAR DIVINATIONS SECTION</u>:

PARADIGMS LOST, AND REGAINED

By Gary Clemenceau

[While the past holds sway over some minds, most in the world live for the future. So, what will said world be like 25 years from now? With this in mind, AcmeVaporware's Night Janitor, Gary Clemenceau, spoke with Dr. John Smallberries, a research fellow at Morvalia Polytechnic University and chairman of AcmeVaporware, and asked him to make a few predictions.]

GC: Dr. Smallberries, what do you see happening in the world in 2025?

DRJ: 2025 will invariably see a complete and utter collapse of 99% of the installed communications infrastructure. This failure will cause end-users to employ an advanced form of Yonder-reaching Echo Location Layer (YELL) vibratory accoustic transport to communicate over indeterminate distances. This form of voice data transport, once the domain of parents and military personnel, will see a resurgence in the average end-user for all forms of mimetic and accusatory transport. Additionally, 2025 will see mainstream implementation of obsolete data packetizing paradigms re-introduced in a variety of physical layer applications. Vermin Area Networks (VANs), once merely a Medieval physical-layer routing solution for pestilence and disease, will be employed extensively across most parts of the world to move data packets in much the same way that data packets move in networks today, only much less efficiently. Already, voles and rats are being tested in several labs -- many without their knowledge, or consent.

GC: I see.

DRJ: Yes, it will be quite exciting.

GC: What exactly is physical layer routing?

[Dr. Smallberries hits the interviewer in the arm.]

GC: Ow.

DRJ: THIS is the physical layer. Routing means address-ing and moving things around, like the mail. The packet is the letter. In fact, the coming physical layer routing Renaissance will ultimately give rise to Bionic Area Networks (BANs). Strangely, examples of this super-charged physical layer packetizing technique exist today. Already in the US, several hundred "volunteer" postal car-riers, injured in "accidents," have already been imbued with bionic technology under the watchful eyes of Rex Mundi, Postmaster General in charge of Super Secret Projects. All surviving postal carriers have fully embraced their new lives and look forward to actually working just like people at other delivery companies. This test-bed introduction of bionic technology should completely eradi-cate the sloth inherent in the old US Postal System. All told, these forthcoming atavistic voice and packet para-digms will continue to enslave people in greater numbers while making them feel empowered.

GC: But what about the average workers in corporate set-tings? How will the future affect them?

DRJ: Ah, the average worker will continue to descend into what we at Morvalia Tech have labeled "The Neo-Dickensian Era." Workers will increase their work days from the current 18-hour day to 19, in an attempt to keep their inflated stock price walls intact. Holidays will be abol-ished and the sun will be regarded as evil.

GC: An interesting viewpoint. What else? What about venture capital? Will it eventually dry up?

DRJ: Actually, I'd expect to see an acceleration of the VC money stream via new CEO money-procurement technologies, as well as a virtual elimination of anything that slows down the process, like PR people.

GC: But what about the immediate future? What's going to happen to the stock market?

DRJ: In time for the real Millennium -- which begins January 1st of the year 2001 -- the market will completely crash to about 1000 points. Utterly despondent, most VCs and CEOs and cube billionaires will leap from their second-story windows and break their legs. While in the emergency room, they'll be on their cellphones selling everything. The market will then collapse to pre-20th Century levels, settling at about 125 points. Fearless elementary school students will then purchase all these stocks in 5 minutes for micro-pennies on the dollar from within their computerized day-trading classrooms, and the market will rebound to 500000 points. This will create an even bigger, younger elite of ten-year-old trillionaires. They will then wander the planet dressed like miniature Edgar G. Robinsons in "The Ten Commandments" toting cigars and sneering at adults. Doves and bunnies will then come seemingly from nowhere and frolic under an immense rainbow. It should be quite an exciting time.

GC: So, invest in healthcare.

DRJ: Yup.

GC: Thanks, doc.

FOR INSTANTANEOUS RELEASE:

ACMEVAPORWARE UNVEILS
NEW GOOGLE-TRAC RAZOR

AVW Ultra-Advanced Psycho-Consumertronics Section
Whips Sheet Off Shocking Personal Grooming System

HIRSUTE, KENTUCKY, August 2, 2006 -- AcmeVaporware
Inc. (AVW) today revealed its new GOOGLE-TRAC Razor
before a horrified, yet good-natured crowd of beauty & bar-

ber science academy graduates. The first overly manic personal grooming system of its type anywhere on earth, the new GOOGLE-TRAC Razor has well over 100 razor-sharp blades that simply don't know when to quit, EVER.

HOW IT WORKS

The first blade comes in and pulls up the whisker a fraction of a millimeter, while the second blade zooms ahead and pulls it up a bit more; the third blade then takes up where the second blade left off, while the fourth blade assists the third, working in unison to hoist the whisker's petard for the deadly FIFTH blade, which helps the sixth do its job, followed by the seventh, eighth, ninth, tenth, eleventh, twelfth, thirteenth, fourteenth, fifteenth, sixteenth, seventeenth, eighteenth, nineteenth, and twentieth blades - that then work in harmony with the next eighty eight blades to FINALLY AND IRREVOCABLY zipzop that pesky growth right off the face of the earth, with extreme prejudice and malice aforethought.

"We decided to stop screwing around and make a serious leap in razor technology profits," said Dr. John Smallberries, president and CEO of AcmeVaporware. "Other personal grooming systems' profits went only just so far. I mean, the American public will believe anything, anyway, so why not?" Dr. Smallberries then unleashed the new GOOGLE-TRAC Razor System on the hundreds of

unsuspecting barber & beauty school graduates. Test subjects' screams were most impressive.

"Our GOOGLE-TRAC Razor System can be used to boost
bottom lines of all types, making it far costlier and more
complicated than more conventional gas-powered solutions," said Dr. John Yaya, Vice President of International
Vice Presidential Systems for AVW. "In contrast, other personal grooming systems are short-sighted, cheap and
kinda suck. Just wait till you see the prices for our
replacement blades! A-HAAHAHAHAHHAHAHA!!!"

"This product has absolutely nothing -- NOTHING -- to do
with Google, which is a FUCKING TRADEMARK OF
GOOGLE," said Google CEO Barney Google. "I'd still love to
have one, of course. Just stop touching me."

About Google

Google Google Google Google Google Google Google Google
Google Google Google Google Google Google Google Google
Google Google Google Google Google, that's all anyone ever
talks about anymore. All your Google Are Belong to Us.

About AcmeVaporware

AcmeVaporware, Inc. is an intergalactic mega-trillion dollar web-based e-powerhouse monstrosity, providing

uncompromising physical layer transport and grooming solutions, pseudo-lexiconographical logistics and torpovapor supply-chain fusion thingies to anyone who will stand still long enough for us to draw an X on their forehead, on a scale that makes the collective armies of all the pharaohs look like a junior high school marching band. Information on AcmeVaporware, its internecine technology and personal grooming system arm, and its future profligate amounts of finest-quality miasma are mostly classified. Regardless, it's all on www.acmevaporware.com anyway, so whatever.

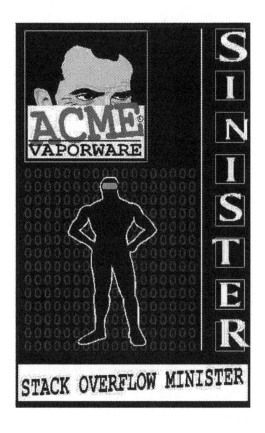

ACME VAPORWARE

SINISTER

STACK OVERFLOW MINISTER

FROM THE AVW KLUNKY OL' E-THING SECTION:

"ASK DR. SMALBERRIES"

[DATE: Removed by Federal Order #FE66438, labeled "CLASSIFIED" and "ew" and "DON'T"]

The following are actual reader questions directed to the shadowy CEO of AcmeVaporware, Inc., Dr. John Smallberries. To ask the good doctor a question, send $10,000 in very large bills to:

Dr. John Smallberries

c/o LANGOSTA GRANDE

Box 666

Mexico City, Mexico

If he uses your question, you'll receive an AcmeVaporware coffee mug suitable for framing, and an autographed picture of Mies van der Rohe. You've been warned, citizen.

Q: Dr. Smallberries, is there a way to quickly eliminate all the system problems associated with my END-USERS?

-Ted in Cleveland, Ohio

A: Interestingly enough, Ted, all networking problems seem to disappear when the end-user vanishes. This is the initial finding of a Morvalia Polytechnic University research study on complex Cauchy-Riemann end-user/WAN administrator interactions. Said findings of this landmark study have caused several carriers to begin adjusting their customer service models to completely alienate and purge all end-users from their systems. This from one SysAdmin: "In the past, we didn't need Franklin Sniffers or complex Gilberto/Habitech sensormatic telltales to let us know when things weren't working in the network. We had 37 million customers for that. But since we've embraced MorvaliaTech's end-user purge, our system up-time hovers in the 100% range. It's very relaxing." You might want to check this out, Ted, and really start living... today.

Q: Doc, my NT MULTI-PROTOCOL ROUTER is hideously spurious and intermittant. I've tried everything, even reinstalling the software. What should I do?

-Brad in San Diego, CA

A: Percussive maintenance, commander. There are precious few system problems that cannot be eradicated with the Networking Ball Peen Hammer of Destiny. The symptoms of a public network in dire need of PM can include: low cranial pressure, chronic javamania, unexplained Hoarkchamber "accidents," boss hauntings, socio-economic ataxia, rampant staff sloth and ennui, a complete and utter lack of winking LEDs, weird buzzing noises around face and head, and a lack of co-worker promiscuity, to name a few. My advice: grip it and rip it.

Q: Dr. Smallberries, in previous studies, ATOMIC RUBIDIUM PACKETS have been successfully sent down fiber, but atomic alkali packets are prone to stick along the way. What can be done about this?

-Tipper Gore, Washington, DC

A: Try helium, Al. In a recent experiment at the Austro-Hungarian campus of MorvaliaTech, atomic helium packets were shot down Percassian fiber. Unlike rubidium and alkali atomic packets, the helium packets flow more smoothly (guided by "evanescent light phlogiston" impinging upon the fibers from an adjacent tachyon reality) since they have first been put into a long-lived excited state which is almost impervious to interactions with the walls of the fiber. Neat, huh?

Q: Dr. Smallberries, RYDBERG PACKET SCULPTING is a new technique for placing data packets in many protocol-energy states simultaneously. Applications could include improved designs for quantum routers, which presently call for collections of rudimentary 2-level quantum data systems, similar to the 2-state (0 and 1) classical binary computers used today. But how could a packet be in, say, 10 protocol-energy states at once?

-Poodle McBride, Nashua, NH

A: Duh. By being whacked by torpolaser pulses of very short duration, of course. Such a pulse is itself really a superposition of sloth-inducing coherent light waves at many different energies. This multi-protocol energy existence is transferred to the packet when it absorbs the torpolaser pulse. Recently, CNN's Wolf Blitzer (a renowned Rydberg packet sculpting fanatic) actively shaped ultra-short laser torpopulses to hit data packets in a beam. This created within the packet what Blitzer calls "wave packet sculpting," a bundle of electron waves dancing in a complex pattern as they go around the nucleus, at times interfering with each other, and making this cool blue light you can read and cook by. Packet interference can already be controlled so carefully that it each node can be used to store several megabits of information, as well as enable a FABULOUS toast experience.

Q: I was wondering if you could help me. I need another alternative to my field-replaceable Frammel packetizing unit for oscillating bridge groncolators. (Niobium or Ytterbium plated preferred). Someone exposed my Frammelstat to UV again and now the unit won't index at initialization.

-Dan Wenderlick, Paris, Texas

A: Ah, we've seen this so many times. As anyone with an advanced degree in TorpoPhysics knows, a Niobium- or Ytterbium-laced oscillation groncolator necessarily needs a properly functioning and field-percussionable Frammel unit (named after Pierre Frammel, the French demolitions engineer and systems administrator) for proper phlogiston yields and indexing. Rest assured that Morvalia Polytechnic researchers have recently turned on the Main TorpoInjector at MorvaLab in Amherst, MA to create a entirely new cruise packet technology that will completely alter the way we think and live. The TorpoInjector is a 580-mile cyclotronesque magnetic racecourse for getting phlogistons up to speed in much greater numbers. This is crucial since oscillation beam intensity is no less important than the energy of collision when producing rare torpo-objects, such as superkindasymmetric torpoparticles (hypothetical hyperinertia- or hypersloth-inducing data cousins of the known phlogistons) and the much sought

Higgs-Feynman (HF) phlogi-boson. New theoretical esti-
mates for the mass of the HF, when matched against
Morvalia Tech's early findings, suggest that Richard
Feynman was right all along, as usual. What does all this
mean? Basically, all needs for field-replaceable Frammel
Units will eventualy dwindle under the crushing wheels of
advanced TorpoPhysical research, giving rise to a seriously deadly cruise packetization. In the meantime, I would
suggest PERCUSSIVE MAINTENANCE, both for the existing Frammel and the guy who exposed it to UV in the first
place, damn him.

*Q: Has sign language ever evolved naturally in any other
community?*

-Timmy Le Marie, Plathp, PA

Sign language has indeed evolved and developed naturally
within communities all over the world, with its sources
extending into prehistory. The best examples seem to exist
on islands. The intersection of old- and new-world cultural vectors are currently being studied by cultural anthro-
pologists investigating areas rife with ancient forms of non-
verbal communication (Manhattan and Sicily being the
most avidly studied). An excellent non-verbal exchange
was recently documented. In one Manhattan alleyway, a
truck driver was unable to move his truck because of a
parked taxi (not "ataxia" as was reported) hindering his
movement. The truck driver leaned out of the window and

invoked an ancient Roman sign with his right hand, middle finger prominent, suggesting that the taxi driver perform a tangential procreative event on himself. The taxi driver, being from Sicily, stepped from his cab and mirrored this exact gesture (thus completing the communication loop) while procuring a baseball bat from behind his seat. The truck driver then resorted to a time-honored, ancient form of violence escalation, pulling a shotgun from within his vehicle and beckoning the other driver to come closer by curling his hand toward his body repeatedly. Alas, the research team's observations were then interrupted by a prolonged fleeing event, with many of the retreating researchers pointing at their heads and rotating their hands in clockwise motions. Needless to say, nonverbal or sign language has been with us a long time, and continues to make our existence a rich -- if not wholly dangerous and limited -- cultural experiment.

AVW BLUNT-FORCE TRAUMA SECTION EXCERPT
FROM A RECENTLY DISCOVERED
BUSH ADMINISTRATION
"PRIMER ON APOCALYPTIC EVENTS"

TITLE: TO THE RIGHT OF GOD

As you all know, the End of the World should come as no surprise, as it has been prophesied by Our Lord Jesus Christ for roughly 2000 years. We in the Bush Administration fully accept God's Terrible & Righteous Judgement & Extreme Wrath upon us -- especially for those who are wicked and deserve it. It can now be freely stated that this Administration's main purpose is to both marshal and concentrate the efforts of all our earthly forces to bring about the End of the World that much more quickly.

The world is, of course, not what it was. Lambs and lions do not walk together peacefully. Man is not nice to his fellow man. Many men and women shun the word of God and lie with one another unnaturally. Many works of art and literature are unholy and profane. In short, many deserve to die. They deserve eternal damnation. They are beasts. They bear tattoos -- the Mark of the Beast. In fact, many of YOU, assembled here, are beasts and deserve eternal damnation. Many of you are Evil -- many in this room -- and deserve an Eternity of Pain and Suffering. It was this Administrations firm guiding hand that helped bring about this pain, this pain you so richly deserve. The Bible tells us that those who are Evil will be cast into the pit -- cast down as quickly as those seers in the Bush Administration will ascend to the Kingdom of Heaven. It is our birthright. So lay you down, you sinners, and take your medicine, because yea, though you walk through the Valley of the Shadow of Death, you are, in a word, Evil. Thus, you who are not with us - both foreign and domestic -- deserve to die in the most horrible way we can accomodate. This has been our purpose. This has been our goal.

Those of you who are not evil, rejoice! The end of suffering is finally at hand! Many are the days we have waited for this moment! Waited for the Ultimate Hand of Our Lord to smote the puny lives and works of Man. But you, like those of us who are just, will finally reap the righteous bounty of what you have sewn. You will stand to the Right of God and look down upon the sinners. But do not pity them. No. Know that it is what they deserved, and that our course was the Right One, and that all means justified the Righteous End, and that Vengeance does not belong to God alone -- but to all of us, His instruments on Earth. Rejoice in Your Newfound Lives of Peaceful Righteousness. And be happy.

Thank you and best of luck.

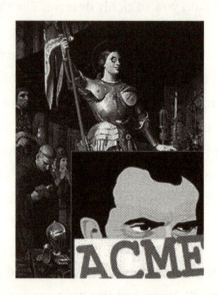

AVW TORPOPHYSICAL NEWS #1011
FROM THE AVW JOURNAL OF
TORPOPHYSICAL PHLOGISTON ADVANCES

THE SPEED OF LIGHT THROUGH CEO CRANIUMS IS INDEPENDENT of the speed of the light and reason through normal braincases. Dr. John Yaya of Morvalia Polytechnic University reaches this conclusion by studying phlogiston emission arriving from distant Powerpoint Presentation Bursters (PPBs) usually associated with intense tradeshow environments.

Consider, he says, the phlogiston production at the PPB event horizon: phlogiston will come to us from the near side of a presumed CEO expanding ego-object, and from the receding far side. Because of expected explosive nature of the PPB engine, its near and far sides might, at least in some cases, be moving apart at a fair fraction of the speed of light, or at least fast enough to make someone behind the blast shield flinch. Any differential in the speed of light arising from these two phlogiston-emitting locations would then result (after a very long press tour) in a stretched-out and prolonged Powerpoint space-time ripple upon arriving at what scientists like to call "the point."

In addition, the emitted phlogiston would scatter off of energetic thermal electrons on leaving the burst sources, further broadening the phlogiston pulses. From the observed sharpness of the arriving pulses, one can deduce the independence of c from the source speed to be less than a part in 10^20, an improvement by a factor of... "let's say a lot" said Yaya, over previous tests of this tenet of CEO point-relativity theory. At last week's Powerpoint Phlogiston Brain-Box Burster Thingie (PPBBBT) committee meeting in Fleagle, NH, Yaya blustered for at least an hour on this topic before they brought out the ham and decided that most presentations were a complete waste of space AND time.

BACK TO SCHOOL?

By Dr. John Smallberries

Social outcasts recall a youthful dread associated with going back to school: riding a bus that smelled of socks; food reminiscent of prison riots; clothes your mom not only picked out, but made you WEAR IN PUBLIC. Imagine merging those sweatered feelings with the impending doom of a fresh Monday morning in Corporate America. What you're imagining is Ayn Rand Elementary School in Woodvale.

On a recent visit, I was faced with what looked to be a Dickensian workhouse, stolidly gray amidst an empty brown field. There were no sounds of children. No scream-ing. No gleeful, maniacal laughter ending with a sudden thud. But SOMETHING was happening inside. I kept catching sounds of an odd clicking.

I was there at the behest of Dr. Eldon Tyrel, principal and CEO of Ayn Rand (known as "The Rand"), who had invited me to see why his new experimental school was the best example of a Silicon Valley elementary.

Inside, I discovered Dr. Tyrel, as well as the source of the clicking noise. Under a broad expanse of fluorescent lighting were hundreds of tiny cubicles. The clicking was coming from the frenzied keystrokes of three hundred little sets of fingers typing furiously.

"The Rand prepares children for life in Corporate America," said Dr. Tyrel, "and allows us to harness the moneymaking potential of youthful energy and creativity *right now*, while we can still use it, before burn-out settles in -- thus bringing new and exciting outsourcing opportunities to valley corporations in dire need of young blood."

Having missed Challenge Period, I'd arrived during First Period: Day Trading, timed to begin as the market opened in New York. It was actually a part of every school period in-between bells, as well. As it was, several of the tykes were already multi-millionaires.

Second Period was devoted to coding. The little ones were

furiously trying to finish some bit of database management code for a large local company that had laid off all its adult workers more than a year previous.

Third Period: Marketing and Public Relations. Some kids worked on their five-hundred-year roadmaps, while others immersed themselves in common-sense development groups, where they touched things that were hot (labeled HOT) and sharp (labeled SHARP). In the PR clinic, kids learned how to suck up to the media and use jargon in place of creativity, as well as bill an hour for five-minutes-worth of work.

The recess bell rang. Serious-looking munchkins streamed from their cubes and snagged Starbucks coffee and cookies laced with antacid; coffee, candy and cigarettes were provided free of charge throughout the day in lieu of milk and water. The recess bell rang again four minutes later.

"Recess used to be five minutes," said Dr. Tyrel, "but we found that extra minute really useful in breaking morale."

Next Period saw children in stock portfolio clinics. Fifth Period dealt with Maximizing Shareholder Value. Sixth Period was normally concerned with learning to jerk around vendors, but today's curriculum was postponed for more coding. (Evidently, there was a big push to get the demo done.)

Seventh Period was a working lunch, with Indian food brought in while the children slaved. Eighth Period: more coding while Dr. Tyrel delivered an inspirational speech over the PA system.

"Besides being a part of history, you lucky children will be the world's first trillionaires. Remember: money is the most important thing... that, and making your deadlines."

Ninth Period involved Financing. Huge smiling pictures of "famous" venture capitalists were displayed, as well as tips on how to spot a useful banker in a crowded room.

Finally, well past dark, the last Period was upon us. Similar to the Challenge Period, the kids were required to sit for an hour in small, fast-moving automobile-like structures chained to each other around a quarter-mile track. Each "car" was equipped with a radio and a fake cellphone. Signs along the "road" identified the scene as a scale model of the south-bound 880. Kids sat and looked miserable in the heat, just like their adult counterparts, and were shown how to eat dinner in their cars while talking on cellphones and working on sourpoint presentations. (The morning class taught how to sleep, eat, shower, shave, apply makeup and read memos during the morning commute.)

In the end, Dr. Tyrel summed up the experience: "We need schools like this to bring kids' high expectations down to earth. After all, the pyramids could never have been built in a democracy."

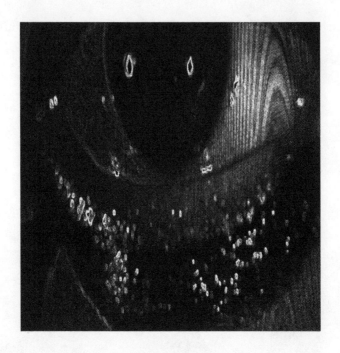

FOR IMMEDIATE RELEASE:

ACMEVAPORWARE & MATTEL PROMISE
FRESH BARBEAN HOLIDAY AVATARS
ON SHELVES BY Q3 NEXT YEAR

AVW Doppelganger Section and Mattel's
Special Barbie Unit Jumpstart Aging Icon
with Unique & Deadly Design;
High-Ranking Ohio Officials Participate in Tests

BELPRE, Ohio, February 16, 2007 - AcmeVaporware, Inc.
today announced that it had joined with Mattel's Special

Supersecret Barbie Plastic Surgery Unit to jumpstart the ailing line of babeticious, impossibly proportioned dolls, providing a much needed infusion of state-of-the-art homunculous jargon to one of the world's largest toymakers. AcmeVaporware CEO Dr. John Smallberries made the announcement from the doorway of his Cessna Citation X before a handful of lecherous dollmakers surrounded on all sides by over 10 million wide-eyed Barbies dragged onto a small airport tarmac for the event.

"It's never too early to start thinking of advanced holiday giftage strategies," said Dr. Smallberries, while toting one of the first jackbooted Klaus Barbies (a gift for Dick Cheney) off the assembly line. "This is, of course, what we're conditioned to think from birth. Preamble notwithstanding, I was in some megalopolis toy store the other day (looking for the Bush Adminsistration's new, 'Land of the Extremely Lost' Sleestak lunchboxes) when I stumbled upon the Barbie aisle. Mattel obviously needed some serious retooling. Boy, are you people in for it." Dr. Smallberries then proceeded to unveil sample Barbies for the one local reporter:

Remember the Alamo Barbie -- Comes with a puzzled-looking Barbie wearing a cowboy hat, leather fringe jacket, and dead Davy Crocket

Polynesian Barbie -- Comes with plastic leis, vial of missionary venereal diseases, and a Martin Denny CD

Copenhagen Barbie -- Tie-dyed clothing replete with candid wildebeest photos and bong

(Un)Grateful Dead Barbie -- (See Copenhagen Barbie)

Gaming Community Barbie -- formerly Pocahontas Barbie; slots sold separately

Redneck Barbie -- Done up with rhinestoned denim skirt, unconscious dawg and half-empty bottles of Southern Comfort; slot machines, singlewide trailerhome and rusting '72 Ford Torino (with grass growing from the engine compartment) sold separately

Manic Barbie -- Wind her up and she stays up for days vacuuming, re-organizing her closets and making "To Do" lists on old Home Pregnancy Test packaging

Freudian Barbie -- Comes naked with a fish, some cigars and an autographed picture of Julie Andrews

Vintage Coder Barbie -- Box verbiage: "Work toward impossible deadlines and circumnavigate HUGE VITRIC EGOS with VINTAGE CODER BARBIE. Learn that ALL you can do is NEVER enough!" Pull her string and she shouts:

"CODE FASTER YOU HOGS! IT'S ALMOST 1999!" Vintage Coder Barbie Accessories include: computer; another computer; an old 486 computer; an older computer; a TRS-80; a picture of Spock; twin carpal tunnel wrist-supports and ergonomic manical/keyboard; tiny tiny gray cubicle; faded old squeezy fuzzy thing; and a calendar highlighting the outdoor life you don't live.

Of course, **Silicon Valley Barbie** was also represented. Accessories include: laptop; another laptop; four color-coded cellphones with dorky futuristic "WIRED" headsets; Palm XB9000 integrated abdominal shunt; 90 bottles of Tums; smelly boxes of four-day-old indian food; 19000 unread email; an old press kit from 1995; a tired Lexus filled with hundreds of sticky, half-full Starbuck's cups and dirty laundry; inch-thick legal contracts and pre-high-lighted charts showing Barbie's declining stock portfolio and schedule ("only 9 more months to 9% vesting!").

Of course, the requisite **Presidential Barbie** (comatose, wealthy, invades everything) and **Congressional Barbie** (comatose, wealthy, allows everything to be invaded) were both on sale for $98,932.13 each, just in time for the end of the fiscal year.

About AcmeVaporware

AcmeVaporware, Inc., is a pangalactic quadrillion-dollar e-powerhouse monstrosity, providing fully compromised layer ONE transport and doll rehab solutions, quasi-lexiconographical logistics and torpovapor demand-chain fission hummers to anyone who will stop taking pictures of us all the time with their goddamn cellphone cameras, on a scale that makes Gilligan's Island look like a sitcom. Information on AcmeVaporware, its fun and springy technology and anthropomorphic avatar arm, and its future profligate amounts of finest-quality MIST are almost entirely classified. Regardless, its all on acmevaporware.com anyway, so whatever.

FOR IMMEDIATE RELEASE:

ACMEVAPORWARE & FOX ANNOUNCE
SUPER ULTRA-X

AVW Xtreme Gaming Section & World's Most Insensate
Media Conglomerate Team to Maim Countless
20-Somethings With Thoughtless Seasonal Line-up;
Future Victims Line-up Around the Block, Sign Away
Rights, Clamor for Abuse

ANY HOSPITAL, USA, March 1, 2007 -- AcmeVaporware, Inc., today announced that it had joined with FOX to create a spate of "extreme sports," labeling them "THE MOST EXTREME SPORTS EVER, FUCKER." The announcement was made before an entire wing of broken and bed-ridden Reality TV and Xtreme sports contestants -- as well as several hundred smiling orthopedic surgeons who invented this stuff in the first place. Lines of iPod-grooving 20-somethings stretched around the block to sign up for future pain and humilation.

Dr. John Smallberries, AVW's notorious Chairman and CEO, began the proceedings as he often does, by quoting Freud: "Dear old Sigmund once wrote: 'Instinctual passions are stronger than reasonable interests.' Anyone who makes liquor runs for Supreme Court justices knows that one. But what do you get when the two are combined? SuperUltra-X, baby." Dr. Smallberries concluded his remarks by stating that Freud needs invoking to understand what drives SuperUltra-X. SuperUltra-X refers to extreme sports, but with a difference that can only be experienced. Here's a short list of events (and filmcrews) coming soon to a township, cable affiliate, or local hospital near you:

SuperUltra-X Hunting Challenge -- In this visceral, thrill-a-minute event, both male and female contestants travel to the northernmost regions of Canada where they are separated from their clothes, forced to rub tuna all over their naked flesh, and tossed out onto the melting icepack with a knife about 4" long to combat a dozen bio-engineered 15-foot-tall polar bears who've been force fed nothing but Marty Stouffer "Wild America" videos. Alternative title: "Red Ice Massacre."

SuperUltra-X Sailing Challenge -- Think America's Cup on the Spanish Main. Boat skippers are intentionally blinded in one eye before unleashing their multi-million-dollar sailing vessels in much the same way as their blood-thirsty America's Cup counterparts. Each boat now bristles with 32 large cannon (16 port and starboard), with a variety of shot (grape, chain and whopper) and scads of black powder charges. The addition of armed boarding parties, planks and intentional ramming promises to make this a most popular event.

SuperUltra-X Baseball Challenge -- Subtitled "Take me out of the ballgame," all the folks in the stands are handed .22 caliber rifles and one bullet as they enter the park. They are encouraged to eliminate anyone for slow play or a lack of performance. A similar system is currently being installed in Florida and U.S. Supreme Courts.

SuperUltra-X Football -- This is simply regular "old-time" ouchie football, though now all the doctors, pain medication, jacuzzis, icing, trainers and huge salaries are removed. All games are scheduled to take place above the arctic circle.

SuperUltra-X Golf -- In what promises to be an entertaining series, this first entry begins in San Quentin Maximum Security Correctional Facility. Golfers must play through the prison with no supervision other than the camera crews (safe in titanium-alloy cages). Be careful picking up your ball, let alone taking a drop in the shower.

SuperUltra-X Living -- TEXAS is the first locale of this very interesting feature. Contestants must live in Dubyaland -- Midland, TX -- in a fire-ant-infested trailer park while all their relatives are simultaneously released from death row to console the contestants after their dot-coms fail. Tequila, Cheetos, bibles, shotguns and machetes will be issued to all entrants. Viewers will be especially keen on Howey Long as the "Mother-in-Law."

SuperUltra-X Travel #1 -- "Drunks across the desert" is the jewel in the crown for the Xtreme series. Five guys are dropped in the middle of the Utah Desert with an old '63 Falcon convertible and two cases of Jack Daniels. They must then consume all of the bourbon and somehow make their way on a pre-plotted course to a far-off destination without being arrested. Anyone who dies during the journey must be strapped to the hood of the car.

SuperUltra-X PSYCHOTIC TEEN Para-Wars -- Two teens pumped full of psychotropic drugs are taken from a mall (hence the drugs), strapped into a single parachute and thrown out of an airplane at 20,000 feet. (The parachute is only built to safely support a single teen, hence the "war" element of this plunging cavalcade of death.) Teens are encouraged to sober up quickly and sever their opponent from themselves and the parachute by whatever means possible while attempting to land safely. Cordless power tools and shaped-charge explosives are popular para-wars weapons. Grand prize is survival and a free t-shirt. (Sequel: **SuperUltra-X Married Couple Breakfast War Challenge.**)

SuperUltra-X Caffeinated Barber Challenge -- An all-out race to see which team of four barbers can give the most traditional straight-razor shaves in the space of an hour after consuming 40 gallons of coffee. Volunteer shavees are encouraged to apply. Free first aid and blemishes removed while-U-wait.

SuperUltra-X Hunter/Jumper Steeplechase -- Specially bio-engineered horses (with two front-facing eyes) turn predator. With sharpened hooves, sharpened teeth and special spiked harnesses, they chase jockeys mercilessly through jumps over flaming pits. "Barb Wire" meets "National Velvet" in the "Thunderdome."

SuperUltra-X Ironman Challenge -- OK, let's see how tough these guys really are. "S.U.X. IRONMAN" adds a radiation poisoning event to the beginning of the swimming, biking and running segments. Contestants also sport leeches during the distance running.

Waste-Hauling Contract Challenge -- Another "reality" contest that follows four young hopefuls seeking to make inroads into the exciting and rewarding sanitation services industry. No "X" required to make this one worth viewing.

SuperUltra-X Batting Challenge -- Rocks, roughly baseball-sized, come flying in at 200 MPH. You get a helmet, a baseball bat, and a cup. Object: DON'T GET HIT. This is the first entry of what will soon be known as "Kinetic Reality" shows.

SuperUltra-X Badminton Challenge -- Here's the second "Kinetic Reality" entry. The shuttlecock is loaded with explosive and rock salt. Minimal clothing worn. If it contacts the ground, BOOM. Volleyball variant.

SuperUltra-X Dating Challenge -- Male "reality show" contestants are dropped into the downtown area of a small midwestern city with no money, no I.D., smelly shabby clothes and temporary oral implants that make coherent speech difficult. Tiny cameras are implanted to their heads, facing forward. The first man to go on a formal date and get laid wins a million dollars. Prostitution is allowed as a way to earn money, but does not qualify as a "win" for the purposes of the competition. The woman must be employed and earning at least $65,000 a year. (NOTE: Get married and forfeit the million.)

About AcmeVaporware

AcmeVaporware, Inc., is a quaint and motherly ubergalactic multi-quadrillion-dollar entertainment juggernaut, providing all sorts of impossible things in all sorts of impossible ways, to anyone who will just HOLD STILL. Information on AcmeVaporware, its teeny, BROBDINGNAGIAN storehouse of technological floob, and its indecent indecencies are wholly classified, except for that smokin' chili recipe. Regardless, its all on acmevaporware.com anyway, so whatever.

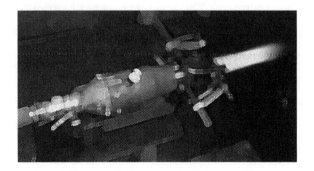

ACMEVAPORWARE TORPOPHYSICS BULLETIN #9989:
FELINE REACTIONS TO TORPOVAPOR PRODUCTS

From the AcmeVaporware Institute of TorpoPhysics

Bulletin of TorpoPhysicalNews

Number 9989, March 14, 2007 by John Baalbeck,

Morvalia Tech, Haughland's Mill, NY;

John Smallberries, UC Santa Yritrea, Yritrea, CA

ABSTRACT

Cats were exposed to photographs of AcmeVaporware torpovapor products. The products were of various sizes, shapes, styles and manners of sloth-inducement. The cats' responses were recorded and analyzed.

FINDINGS OF PRIOR INVESTIGATORS

John Patrick Shanley (1958) found inconclusive results

in studying feline reactions to pre-miasma product families. John O'Connor and John Picklechmuusen (1990)
found inconclusive results in studying feline reactions to
early Casperiteä test heads. John Ooomph (1965) found
inconclusive results in studying feline reactions to high-
sensitivity photophlogiston detection. John Stugelmeyer
(1955) found inconclusive results in studying feline reactions to nanotransscopic silicon data (well before this
industry ever really existed). John Maxxillofacialattic
(1986) found inconclusive results in studying feline reactions to atomic-resolution NTMS vapordata imaging.
Other related studies (John Johnson 1972, Caligari 1987,
Schwartzenbunger 1983) have since been retracted
because the investigators were not able to reproduce their
results. All researchers had been operating on U.S.
Government "BlackWorld" grants and have since turned
up missing or dead, per Federal Order #FO133-900869,
subset "A."

John Wharfen (1988) performed a series of experiments
in which cats were exposed to photographs of AVW CKO,
John Yaya, a man whose many patents include all
Stanislau Vacuum internal parts and fugitive evaporative
network sloth exciminators, which glean data remaining
in the vapor path of the recention bridge-hose. After viewing the John Yaya photograph, 26% of the cats exhibited
paralysis of the legs and body, including the neck. An
additional 31% of the cats exposed to the Bork photo-

graph showed other types of severe neurological and/or pulmocardial distress and/or exhibited extremely violent behavior. Because of this, we did not include a photograph of this AcmeVaporware corporate officer in our study.

MATERIALS

Five photographs were used in the study. The photographs (please see below for list) display a range of different types of Torpovapor products, described as inducing sloth at any given distance (i.e., torpometric). Previous research has shown that ALL felines exhibit inherent torpo-qualities, though this has been ascribed to torpovapor leakage in small appliances and preternatural mother-in-law/small children exigencies.

The test subjects were male cats (females burst into flame, as a group), all between the ages of four and six. 229914 cats participated in the study. Three cats exploded in Franklin/Purr episodes during the study due to causes unrelated to the torpovapor products. Fifteen cats gave birth while viewing the photographs. This is not seen as significant.

METHODS

Each cat was exposed to the photographs. One photograph was shown at a time. Each photograph was visible for a span of twenty seconds. The photographs were presented in the same order to each cat.

While each cat was viewing the photographs, it was held by an AcmeVaporware laboratory assistant (shown below in special cat-resistant suit developed by NASA). To ensure that the cats were not influenced by stroking or other unconscious cues from the assistant, the assistant was anesthetized prior to each session. The cats' reactions were assessed for changes in pulse rate, respiration, eye dilation, fur shed rate and qualitative behavior.

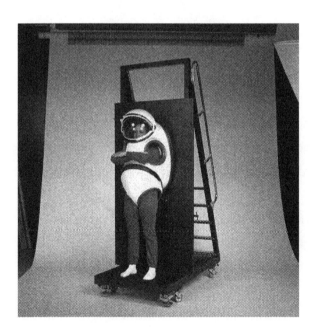

NOTE #1: cat consciousnesses were not augmented by any form of psychotropic drug or hallucinogen.

NOTE #2: no cats were intentionally harmed during the course of these tests; however, four AcmeVaporware interns were hospitalized with serious feline-related claw "burn-out" wounds suffered during the course of the testing. Warning: Mackeral Tabbys (orange) and Siamese were found to be especially lethal.

RESULTS

The results are presented in Table 1. The quantitative results are average values calculated over the entire feline subject population. The qualitative results are broken out by percentages of the subject population.

The following products were shown to the felines (please reference the AcmeVaporware product family for detail):

1. Idaho Vacuum-Assist Reticulator Nozzle for Gilberto, Schlumberger and Habitech Mainline Systems
2. Omaha Rinconston-vaned HoarkChamber
3. Madison "Break-away" Bi-valve Chamber Obstruction
4. "John Bob-Jones" Splash Ferrule Blast Reticulator
5. Cuyahoga Network Content Flo-Equalizer.

TABLE 1

Pulse Rate:

* Idaho Vacuum-Assist Reticulator Nozzle: +42%
* Omaha Rinconston-vaned HoarkChamber: unchanged
* Madison "Break-away" Obstruction: +87%
* Splash Ferrule Blast Reticulator: +2%
* Cuyahoga Network Flo-Equalizer: unchanged

Respiration:

* Idaho: +186%
* Omaha: unchanged
* Madison: +317%
* Splash: +3%
* Cuyahoga: unchanged

Eye Dilation:

* Idaho: +83%
* Omaha: +1%
* Madison: +31%
* Splash: +3%
* Cuyahoga: unchanged

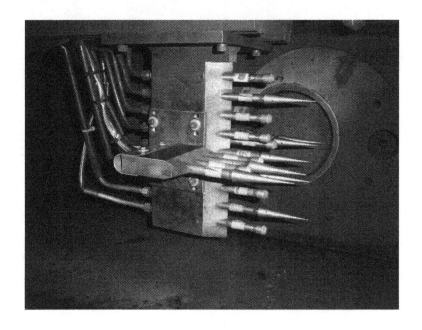

<u>Fur Shed Rate</u>:

* Idaho: +12%
* Omaha: unchanged
* Madison: +19%
* Splash: +2%
* Cuyahoga: unchanged

[Note: the assembled scientists stopped the tests and argued for 2.4 days over whether felines possessed "hair" or "fur." To date, a rift still exists, and several key feline researchers (those that survived) have yet to achieve a complete level of torpofolicular conceptualization.]

Qualitative Behavior:

Idaho:

* 52% attacked photograph; hissing; spitting;
generally agitated behavior
* 34% inverted, fled at high speed
* 14% had no visible response.

Omaha:

* 2% attacked photograph
* 1% fled
* 1% licked photograph, inverted
* 94% had no visible response.

Madison:

* 79% attacked photograph; hissing; generally violent,
agitated behavior; chaotic tail twitch; screeching; spitting;
incontinence
* 17% fled
* 2% inverted and lay inert for days and days
* 2% had no visible response.

Splash:

* 6% attacked photograph
* 1% fled
* 1% stretched, inverted, and pined for the fjords
* 91% had no visible response.

Cuyahoga:

* 100% No visible response.

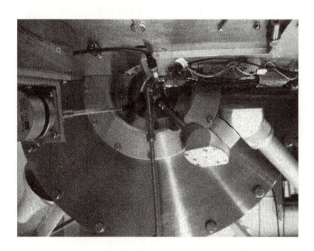

INTERPRETATION

1. Cat sloth was severely impacted/eliminated by AVW Idaho or Madison bi-valve torpovapor products

2. Cat sloth was increased or nominalized by Omaha, Splash ferrule and Cuyahoga torpovapor products

3. Cats are confused and/or disturbed/inverted by unassuming bald men with several advanced torpophysical degrees (as evidenced by feline reaction to John Yaya).

These interpretations are not categorical, but have been cataloged. They are subject to several obvious qualifications. This study did determine that all cats are insane, and/or demon-possessed, yet exhibit loveable tendencies that increase/decrease human sloth and cat-food purchasing at various degrees of separation.

BIBLIOGRAPHY

1. Shanley, John Patrick, "Cat Reactions to Harmonies Produced by Torpomanic Inducing Farm Machinery," in Western Musicology Journal, March/April 1958, vol. 11, no. 2, pp. 4-21

2. O'Connor and Picklechmuusen, John, "Feline Responses to Extraneous Torpovapors," in Midwestern Sociological Review, January 1986, vol. 32, no. 1, pp 51-79

3. Ooomph, John, "Feline Responses to High-sensitivity Photophlogiston Detection," in Urban Sociology Review, November 25, 1987, vol. 21, no. 36, pp. 302-321

4. Hog, John Winthrop, "Feline Torpo-Reactions to Supreme Court Nominees," in Journal of Feline Forensic Studies, vol. 12, no. 8, August 2006, pp. 437-450

5. O'Connor, John, Y., "Feline Responses to Nanotransscopic Silicon Data," in Journal of Silicon Trauma, May 30, 1969, vol. 42, no. 17, pp. 309-324

6. Quoober, John, "Cat Responses to U.S. Government "BlackWorld" Projects," in Torpovatria Proceedings Monthly, May 1975, vol. 3, no. 5, pp. 251-262

7. Schwartzenbunger, John, "A Study of How Cats Respond to Really Weird Things and Vacuum Cleaners," in Hair/Mind/Body/Review, December 1983, vol. 3, no.12, pp. 25-108

8. Seuss, Dr. John, "Feline Responses to Hats & Torpometric Ataxia," in Veterinary Developmental Studies, July 1955, vol. 32, no. 7, pp. 54-62.

Support Torpodata Feline Recovery projects in your own neighborhood. Use duct tape. Cats LOVE duct tape.

[Note: the above piece was based on an original piece penned by Marc Abrahams (marca@chem2.harvard.edu), chief guru editor guy for the Annals of Improbable Research (AIR) in Cambridge, MA. We believe a tank was also named for him. However, we're still not sure if Marc likes ham. Also note: AIR is NOT a puppet information vehicle of Morvalia Tech University. The rumors are simply not true. We were never here. You never saw us.]

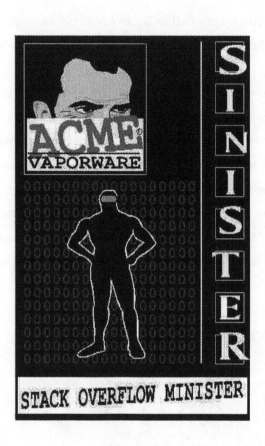

About the Authors

About Dr. John Smallberries

Dr. John Smallberries is Chairman and CEO of AcmeVaporware, Inc., a pioneer in state-of-the-art Nano-Torpometric Networking Subsystems (NTNS) and smoked ham supply chain management. Using vapor lithography and phlogiston etching techniques, Dr. Smallberries was the first to fabricate a 1x1x10-nm suspended beam of transsilicon data which oscillated at an estimated frequency of 7 million THz, while smoking a Virginia ham. Such a resonator will eventually be used in Torpowave Signal Processing (TSP) for off-modulating or de-filtering pulsed data across many thousands of kilometers (see Nature, 12 March 1998), a significant boon to "e-restaurants."

Additionally, Smallberries has over 60 years experience in TorpoSystems, with special emphasis on high-sensitivity smoked-meat photophlogiston data substrates. A former general manager of TNP CABAL/HyperData, Inc., Smallberries has been the key industry leader in magnetic T-Resonance Torpoforce Microscopy in Nondisposable Foodstuffs. Prior to that, he held various senior management and R&D positions at APSX, DARPA, and Morvalia Polytechnic University. Smallberries holds a BSEE in Torpoforce Data Microscopy from MIT, and a PhD in Advanced Exo-Vapor TorpoPhysics from Morvalia Tech.

About Gary Clemenceau

Gary Clemenceau is not nearly so impressive. He spent a scant fifteen years trapped in a Corporate American gulag before releasing himself on his own recognizance, and giving up human flesh almost entirely. During that rather icky, yoked tenure hauling feed wagons for THE MAN, Clemenceau founded AcmeVaporware and spent the next ten years getting fired a lot. He is also author of a work of bizarre, "Corporate Fantasy & Horror" fiction, entitled: *Banker's Holiday -- A Novel of Fiscal Irregularity,* and something else but we can never remember. To date, his first singular novel has caused well over a thousand Incredibly Strange Creatures and Mixed-up Zombies to Quit Their Silly Corporate Day-jobs and Start Living in interesting and satisfying ways. Could be a coincidence.

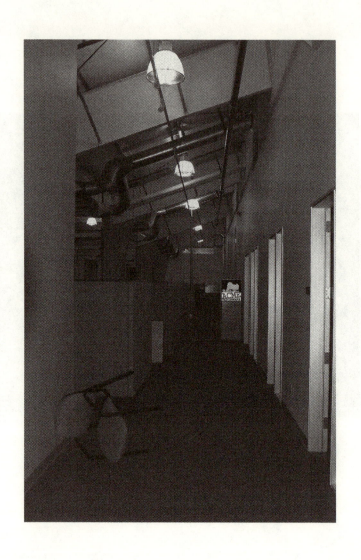

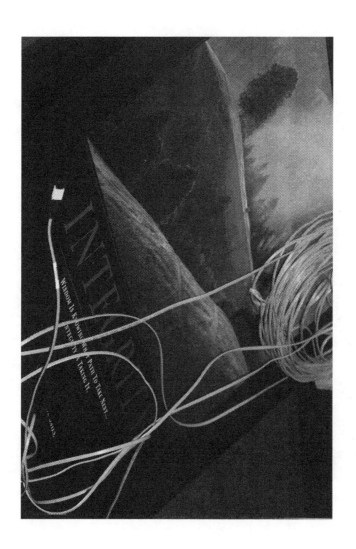

INTRO...

Wisdom Is Knowing What Path To Take Next...
Integrity Is Taking It...

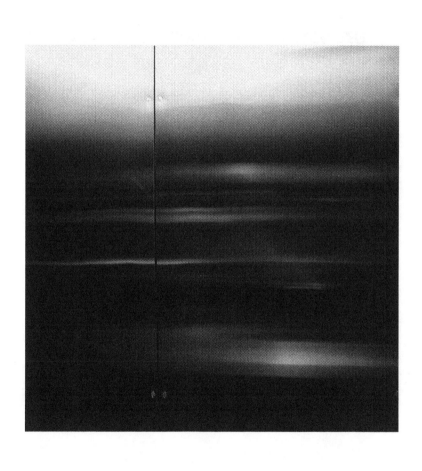

www.ingramcontent.com/pod-product-compliance
Lightning Source LLC
Chambersburg PA
CBHW051228050326
40689CB00007B/839